LOOKING FORWARD

AS

THE

JOURNEY

CONTINUES

GEORGE MILLS

ISBN: 979-8-88945-409-0 (paperback)
eISBN: 979-8-88945-410-6

Brilliant Books Literary
137 Forest Park Lane Thomasville
North Carolina 27360 USA

Printed in the United States of America

NEW
ADVENTURE

As I sit here all alone at the ocean dock, waiting for the time to come for the ship to set sail back out upon the open sea. I recall a time when we once talked about our dream of finding our soulmate in this journey in which we have found ourselves to be on. I'm sure you must have found your heart's dreams here in this deserted town. For you are no longer beside me awaiting to board the ship. What else am I to think?

I can only say, I do have some new memories now to take with me as I start my new adventure in life out on the open sea. Bound unto where? I don't know for certain. For it now appears that the ocean is wild open as it can be for someone like myself who is now, once again, single and free to come and go as he so chooses.

Just one of the fond memories of you is the night you asked if we could take a walk down by the ocean in the moonlight, and you began to sing the most beautiful song my ears had ever heard. I must say, you have a voice that can bring the waves of the ocean to a halt in midair like that night, not so long ago. As for myself, I must continue to move on out with the waves of the ocean, where the ship once again will set sail. But I can only now remember the beautiful smile she once had on her innocent sweet face, like that day she sashayed into the room, taking my breath away, like I had been hit by a hurricane that morning, long ago. Your beautiful smile will be forevermore remembered in my heart, no matter where this life journey may take me.

I feel there something going on in the air. I look up at the ship, only to see the workers coming down the stairs. I go over to where they are and ask, "What is going on?"

One began to tell me, "The captain orders us off the ship, for there is a storm beginning to brew out on the ocean."

Now I had to go and say the word, "Hurricane."

"Right." And now he is telling me there's a storm brewing. Man, I am telling you, if my life gets any better than this, I just don't know what I'm going to do with myself.

I asked him if the captain had said just how long it would be before the storm gets here. He replied, "No, sir, he did not. He only said we would be here until the all-clear is given." I go aboard the ship to see the captain and ask if he knew just how long it may be before he would set sail.

"Sir," he replied, "as for now, I have no answer for you. I'm sure you know how storms are. They very unpredictable."

"Thank you, sir."

I leave and take a walk along the ocean front, as I have done so many times before, just to think about where I have been in my life's journey. I'm standing here, listening to the waves.

I remember a time when I was about ten years old and it was squirrel season. Some friends and I decided to go hunting one afternoon. I didn't own a gun. I asked my brother if I could borrow his that day to hunt with.

We are now in the woods across the road in front of the house. I see a squirrel that I'm going to shoot at. I raise the gun and get the squirrel in my sights. I pulled the trigger. "Oh." Little did I know that the gun had a knockout punch. It put me into a one eighty and set me on my backside. Yes, you can say the squirrel got lucky that time. I never had a gun kick that hard before, nor did I shoot at any squirrels with that gun again that day. That one shot put an end to my hunting.

Well, time has moved on in years, and I'm older and own my own gun. A friend of mine asked if I would like to go coon hunting with him. So I go over to his house. He lives on a farm with cows. Well, around the field, they had an electric fence to help keep the cows from getting out. We had to cross the fence to get back into the woods to hunt. On the front side, they had a gate, but on the backside is where the problem came about. The fence ran along the tree line, and if you didn't know exactly where to look, you would get caught up in it.

Well, we get across with no problem going in, but coming back out did not go so well for me. We were talking and I was not watching where I was going. He said something. I looked over at him and I stepped right into the electric fence. I guess he was trying to tell me, "Look out for the electric fence, your big dummy, that you are about to step into." It felt like I had been attacked by millions of fire ants.

I have more childhood memories about electric fences back before we moved back to my birthplace. The people who owned the house we were living in at the time, also had cows. The house sat in an open field, and the owner decided one day that he was going to put some cows on the land. So, he puts up this electric fence. Being kids and not knowing just what one would do to something. Mom had this dog that I do believe she loved with all of her heart. We were out playing and I let my brothers talk me in to pushing Mama's dog into the fence to see what would happened. I tell you what happened, Mom came out of that house wanting to know what was wrong with her dog. Yes, all fingers pointed to me, for I pushed him into the electric fence.

Mama said, "Come here, boy, you need to go across the road and get me a limb. I'm going to show you what it feels like to be thrown into an electric fence." I'm not going to say just what else I did before this took place. I will say this: she didn't spare the rod. She taught me a lesson of respect I will never forget.

Well, I guess, I could walk on in to town to see my friend at the motorcycle shop. Maybe he has some work that I can do until the storm passes and the ship can, once again, try to leave. I get to the shop, only to find he is closed for the day. For just once in my life, I would like for something to go the way I had planned it. I can only say that God knows the true way such things go in my life.

Well, I must truly say that I really don't feel like being around anyone today. Right now, I feel as if my world is coming down all around me, just like it did three years ago when the one I thought was to be my one and only true love for life, told me she didn't love me any longer. Those words cut my soul in half, not understanding just what one has done wrong. My world came to an end as I once knew it. I ask, within myself, *How can one just up and stop loving someone, and this is even possible?* A question with no answer known to mankind. I know there are millions of excuses to why one might say such a thing as this, but those excuses do not answer the true question which has been asked. I'm thinking of maybe just walking back down to the ocean and consider the living words.

> And ye have respect to him that weareth the gay clothing, and say unto him, sit thou here in a good place, and say to the poor, Stand thou there, or sit here under my footstool: Are ye not then partial in yourselves, and are become judges of evil thoughts? Hearken, my beloved brethren, Hath not God chosen the poor of this world rich in faith, and heirs of the kingdom which he hath promised to them that love Him? But ye have despised the poor. Do not rich men oppress you, and draw you before the judgment seats? Do not they blaspheme that worthy name by the which ye are called? If ye fulfil the royal law according to the scripture, Thou shalt love thy neighbor as thyself, ye do well. (James 2:3–8, KJV)

I have put some thought into what I've just read here, for these thoughts are mine alone. I feel that the one who wrote this is saying to me that we should not judge one another by the richest or by the poorest positions one may own.

With this in my mind, I reflect in remembrance of when I first wrote. The wealth you may or may not have does not teach one the true value of love and respect for one another. Why does one think that one is much better than anyone else? Do they not understand that, in God's eyes, one is no better than the next person who may or may not have accepted Jesus Christ as their personal savior in their life? God gave us all our own special abilities to serve him in a way to glorify him.

Do you recall the three servants who were given talents by their master? Why would one look down their nose at someone else who does not have the same abilities that another may possess. For I asked of you to forgive me for my failures and imperfection as God has forgiven you, your failures and accepted me for who I'm trying to be, changing me not. God has molded me the way he wants me as He has you.

Now it has gotten late, and the sun once again begins to descend over the ocean to close out this sad lonely day here in this old desert. As I make my way to the house, I hear, in the far distance, what sounds to be thunder coming through the soft warm breeze from off the ocean. I look back at the ocean, only to see the rain coming in behind me. I pick up my pace to make it to the house before the rain gets to shore. I get back just in time, only to see her and the older son sitting in the swing, laughing and holding hands. I ask, "How are you two doing tonight?"

They look at me with a look on their faces as if to say, "Why are you asking?"

I'm thinking, *Okay, maybe I should not have asked them anything.*

I go on in and have a nice big cup of hot black coffee. As I sit here, drinking my coffee and listening to it rain, I remember back, as a little boy, to the old house we once lived in. It had a tin roof, and when it would rain at night, it was like taking a sleeping pill. Oh, one could sleep like a newborn baby with that sound.

I'm going to say good night to you all, and get cleaned up and ready for bed, for tomorrow will bring a new adventure, I'm sure, if it be in God's will for us all. For it is by His love and mercy alone that we able to breathe and our hearts beat. Without Him, this could not be at all possible. Goodnight, and sleep well, my friend. Remember, God loves you.

DAYS BEFORE
THE STORM

I start my day like always. Yes, it will be with a big cup of hot black coffee. But for some reason, to me, this morning feels quite different than any before. For the life of me, I just can't put my finger on what it could be right now. "Oh well, maybe it will come to me later as the day goes on."

I'm thinking about going back down to the dock to see the captain, just to see if he has any update as to when the storm is to be coming in. As I make my way to the ship, I see the captain going into this restaurant. So, I proceeded to follow him into the restaurant. "Good morning, Captain. How are you?"

"Good, thank you. How about you?"

"Oh, I'm doing okay. Thank you for asking, sir. Captain, may I ask, do you have the latest update as to when the storm is to make landfall?"

"Sir," he replied, "have a seat. I'll buy you a cup of coffee and we'll talk about the storm."

"Okay, thank you. I would like a cup coffee."

He began to tell me that he is not sure if the storm is coming in our direction or if it's going in a different direction for now. "I haven't been back aboard the ship this morning to check on the latest update, but as soon as I find out anything, I will let you know."

"Thank you, sir, and thank you for the coffee. Hope you have a great day."

Now I leave and head to see my friend down at the motorcycle shop to see if he needs any help in preparing the store for the storm. I get to the store and find that he has got some new bikes that need to be put together. Hey now, this is right up my alley. I love mechanic work. My stepdad taught me, as a young boy growing up, how to work on vehicles.

As I am standing here, looking around, he walks in. "How are you today?" he asks. "I figured you'd be on the ship that was supposed to be leaving this morning."

"No, sir." I begin to tell him about the storm that is beginning to brew out on the ocean.

"Oh, I see," he said. "What! Did you just say there's a storm headed this way?"

"No, sir, but there is a storm that is beginning to brew out on the ocean. I don't know if it's going to come this way or not. All I know is that the captain said he can't leave right now because of this storm. I just came by to see if you might have any work I could be doing."

"I do," he says, "if you know how to put some of these bikes together."

"Well, I do know some, but not a lot about putting motorcycles together, sir."

"Okay, I will let you help me on one and I'll see just how well you work."

"Thanks, sir. I will try my best."

As we get started on one, about half-way into it, he asks, "Would you like a cup of coffee?" I find myself thinking, for the second time since, I've been here in this desert, about the stronger drink he has so many times asked me about, and if I would like to have one.

With last night on my mind, I feel it might be the only thing that will numb the pain, that I feel deep down in my soul. I hear him once again ask, "Would you like a cup of coffee? If you don't, might I ask what you were thinking about?"

"Oh, I'm sorry sir. It's nothing, nothing at all. Yes, I would love a cup of coffee, thank you." He gets up and goes and gets us a big cup, and sits it down on the table.

"Here's yours," he says. "Now, are you going to tell me what's on your mind, son? You have not been yourself today."

"Whatever do you mean, not myself?"

"Well, you normally come in all happy with a smile and a cheerful spirit, but today, there's something different about your attitude."

"Oh, I see what you are saying. It's just the way things seem to be playing out in my life right now. There is nothing going the way I was hoping for."

"What are you saying?" he asked.

"Well, first, the ship can't leave because of the storm, and I guess, with last night on my mind and all."

"Just what took place, if you don't mind me asking?"

"Well, when I got back to the house from the dock, I find her sitting in the swing with the older gentleman's son, laughing and holding hands. I asked, 'How are you two doing to night?' And they looked at me with a grin on their face, like, 'Why do you ask?' I'm thinking, now the son is wanting to say to me, 'Now who's got the beautiful woman? She may have come here with you, but now she is all mine.'"

"Oh, I'm sorry to hear this, my friend. Just what are you going to do?"

"Well, I'm not sure right now. Just what can one do? I know that I'm not wanting to stay there with them any longer in his house. May I ask you, sir, do you have a room here? I can rent just until the ship leaves."

"Well, yes, I do, but I'm not going to charge you any rent. You can pay me by helping me out some here in the shop."

"Thank you, sir, I do appreciate it and I promise I'll work hard to repay you, for allowing me to stay here. You are a kind man in doing so." We finish our coffee and I tell him that I was going to head back to the house to get my things. "I should be back in an hour or so."

"Okay," he replies, "take your time. I will wait here until you get back before I lock up the shop."

THE LONGEST WALK

I meet up with the captain on my way back to the house to pick up my bags. He began to tell me that the storm has now become a category three hurricane, and they are now predicting it to be headed in our direction. "Thank you, Captain, for the update," I say. I'm now thinking just what one would do in a situation such as this. I have never been in a hurricane that has come upon a desert land before.

I go on to the house to pick up my personal things. As I make my way in to the house, I see that they all are sitting around the table, talking. She asks, "Where have you been all day, if you don't mind me asking?"

"I've been in town for most of the day. I just came back to pick up my things, for I'm now going to be staying with a friend until the ship leaves." I go on in to the room to get my bags.

She follows me to the room, only to ask, "Why are you leaving now?"

Once again, I just can't find the words within my heart to explain to this beautiful brown-eyed lady how I'm feeling right now. All I can do is recall the memories that we had made since we first met. But as I softly gaze into her beautiful brown eyes, knowing that they will surely hypnotize me, making it that much harder. I said to her, "I just can not stay here any longer."

As I'm telling her this, I feel my own heart as it begins to cry once again for her warm beautiful love that she has locked up deeper than any man should as I could ever dream of going. Then I remember that she once said she did not know if we could ever be together as one under the Canopy of Heaven. Oh, I find my heart begin to fill with tears once again. "I must go now before my heart drowns from within its own tears for your sweet innocent love. I feel, if the two of you are going to be together as one here under the canopy of heaven, he is going to be the most blessed man in this old desert."

As I make my way back to the shop, it starts to thunder and lightning even more than before. I make it back to the shop just as it starts to rain. He shows me the room where I'm going to be staying until the ship leaves. I put my bags down and go back into the shop to where he is. We started talking about the storm. I was telling him that the captain said the storm is now headed in our direction. All at once, there comes a rumbling of a great roll of thunder. It startled me to the point that I almost fell off the stool, and he begins to laugh.

"By your laughing at me, it reminded me of a time when I was four or five years old. I was watching my favorite TV show, Daniel Boone. It was all thunder and lightning as it is now. Well, Daniel was out hunting."

"Hunting what?" he asked.

"I don't know. I guess for a deer. Now are you going to let me tell my story?"

"Oh sorry, my bad. Go ahead with your story, son."

"Thank, you. Now he sees this turkey."

"What, you said he was hunting a deer!" he says.

I look at him. "Really."

"Oh sorry."

"Now he raises his gun to shoot at this turkey and he pulls the trigger."

"Did he get this turkey?" he asked.

"Oh my, please. Come on, now."

"Well, I'm just asking."

"Yes, you would ask before I got done. Now, as I was about to say, he fires his gun. All I saw was a bright light and then everything went black. I fell back off the stool. I thought at the time that I had been shot, only to find out, after everyone had stopped laughing at me for falling off the stool like you just were, that the T.V. had got struck by lightning."

"Well, did he get his turkey or not?"

"I don't know, for when the lighting struck the TV, it blew up. No more TV or Daniel Boone, okay."

He asks, "Would you like to have that strong drink now?"

"No thanks, sir. I am thinking that, I will just go on to bed. Goodnight. See you tomorrow."

ONE STORMY NIGHT

I t's one stormy night, here in this desert. We had said good night and I went on to bed, only to find myself unable to sleep, for the thunder and lightning kept me awake. I get up and go into the shop and fix myself a cup of coffee and a bite to eat. As I sit here, drinking my coffee, I begin to reflect on a time long ago, to when I first wrote this notice for one of the most beautiful wildflowers that I had ever laid eyes on.

On a warm summer morning, as I sit here on the steps, drinking my coffee and enjoying the warm breeze, I notice a rose as it begins to blossom. It reminded me of the first time I saw your sweet innocent face when it develops a smile. If only you knew how your beautiful smile alone could give one's fading heart the breath of new life.

I can only hope in my prayers, when I leave this journey of life that the one who is standing by my side will share their beautiful smile. Only to know, in my fading heart, by their smile alone, that there is a life forevermore awaiting me in their Father's kingdom.

Oh, how I'd love to be able to, once again, gaze softly into those baby-brown eyes of yours. I feel my heart begin to fade from the tears that my eyes have released. I know that just the warmth alone from your sweet innocent smile would bring comfort to my fading heart, drying the tears away.

For now, your smile has only become a sweet memory I will hold, forevermore, in my fading heart. Oh Lord, hear my heart's cry once more, show me the way unto her heart, that she may see my heart cries for one's love such as her.

Oh Lord thy God, do hear one's heart's cry, I'm asking of you. For you have said, "Ask and you shall receive, knock and it shall be opened". Oh, Lord, I ask of you to let her find, within her own tear-stained heart, her way clearly unto my heart. For my heart is fading fast for a love such as hers. To share our love with each other in the good times, as well as in the bad times, as ones who are living their lives together under the canopy of your heavenly kingdom here on earth. Oh, Lord. Just how does one find their one and only true love, which you have created them to have together and to cherish one's love for another? In sharing their sweet memories of love together as they journey through life. As it stands now, oh Lord, you know, I can only dream my dream of one day being able to stand before her and softly gaze into her beautiful baby-brown eyes and tell her how much her love truly means to someone such as me, and how much I would love for her to rest her love upon my heart, for them to beat as one together under the Canopy of Heaven. Just to be able to caress her soft rosy cheeks and touch her rose-red lips with mine. Is it just one's dream of such a love as her? Does one's love such as this even exist?

"Oh Lord, does a love such as hers only live in my dreams? Oh Lord, was my first true love only a dream in which I have awoken from, only to find myself all alone? Oh Lord, only you know if the dream I dream will come true, or is to just a dream that can't come true? Is this life I'm living only just a dream that one can't be awakened from? I say, only you know if this is just a dream or not. Oh Lord thy God in Heaven and Earth, and of the universe that surrounds me, only you know the true meaning of this life in which you have created me for you own sole purpose. For only in your time, oh Lord, will it be done according to your own free will. So I only ask of you, my Lord, for you to keep my feet on the right path which you have placed before me, oh Lord, so, that these eyes of my heart will stay focused upon worshipping you.

THE SHELTER BENEATH THE EARTH

I hear something. I turn to see what it could be. There he stood with some other people at the door, trying as hard as he could to get the door unlocked. I go over to help from within to open it. "The storm is now upon us", he said as they all came in. "Follow me, we must seek shelter." he says, as he runs over to this bookshelf.

I'm thinking to myself, *Now, how is this bookshelf going to provide any shelter for these people?* Little did this old country boy know that this was not your ordinary bookshelf. I also did not know what was about to happen next. He reaches and pulls one of the books that was on the bookshelf, and it begins to open. No, not the book itself, okay? Behind this bookshelf was a set of stairs leading down into, what appeared to me, one of the most beautiful mansions built beneath the surface of this earth.

In all the chaos that was going on at the time, I didn't realize that the family with whom I was previously staying with was amongst the people that came in with him. I started looking around for her, and didn't see her. I start to go over to the counter to fix a cup coffee. As I do, I see someone walk out of this other room. It was her. I go on over to counter and get a cup coffee and sit down on the barstool.

My mind begin to reflect to the time, when I first met her at that old cactus. She came riding upon the camel's back, that day, like a beautiful goddess. That day will live in my memories forevermore. Oh, how her warm soft silky skin felt when I laid my weary head upon her shoulder, covering my face with her long silky hair blocking the hot sun from off my face. Well, once again, I find myself beginning to feel weary from lack of sleep. I'm going to say goodnight here and try to get some much needed rest. May God keep his hands around us on this stormy night.

A new day has come about here in the mansions beneath the earth's surface. I smell the aroma of food being cooked. I get up and go in to the kitchen to where the food is being prepared, and there she stood, as beautiful as one could ever be in my dream. I ask, myself from within my heart, could this also be just a dream in which I have not truly awakened from? If this is only just a dream, then I don't want to be awoken from within it. For within this dream, just maybe, she will find it within her own heart to see her way clearly, unlock her divine love, and let it flow upon me like the heavenly rains.

She says, "Good morning," in her soft angelic voice. "How did you sleep, and would you like to have something to eat?"

"Well, yes, thank you for asking."

"What can I fix for you?" she asks.

"What I would love to have today is some good old butter grits and eggs, bacon, and some of Mom's good homemade buttermilk biscuits. She could make the best homemade biscuits ever. I can remember, when I was growing up, she would cook them every morning. I would be the first one up and dressed, just to be the first one to the table to eat them homemade biscuits of hers, along with some homemade cane syrup. I would poke a hole in the center of the biscuit and put the cane syrup over in it, now that was some good eating. Oh, how, I am missing, you, Mom and Dad. May you both rest in peace with our Heavily Father until we are together again. Love you both always. Your son."

"Sorry," she said. "Can't help you there."

"Oh well, I'll just have what you are having. It sounds delicious."

"Yes, I know, for there's no one that can cook like Mom."

As we were eating, she came right out and asked, "Why did your mom and dad give you the name that they did?"

"Well, they would not be the ones who gave me my name."

"Who, then, named you?"

Well, it's like this. Mom told me, that, four months before I was to be born, my great-grandmother was laying on her deathbed. Mom was sitting there beside her, and she reached over and laid her hand upon Mom's stomach and told her that she was going to give birth to a son. She was to give me this name and that she would have one more son after me and then two daughters. So I will say my great-grandmother named me, who I never got to meet. She had to be the sweet wildflower in this world, outside of Mom of course, because Mom said she was the one who taught her how to cook them homemade biscuits and tomato gravy and how to make homemade butter. She cooks some of the best cornbread to go with the purple peas and lima beans. She would put a ham hock and some okra over in the peas and just let them cook for an hour or so. I would take the cornbread and crumble it up with the peas. Man, you talk about something good. Now that was good. Okay, now I will have a cup of your coffee. That is, if you don't mind?

Well, you ask, how do I know Mom could make homemade butter? It may have been a year or so after they sold my horse that Mom bought her a milk cow. She would take the cream from off the mike and make butter. If you have never had yourself some home-made butter, I must say, you have been missing out on some of the best things in life.

Well as we were talking, in came the gentleman who owned the motorcycle shop. We say good morning. She asks him if he would like something to eat.

"Well yes, I would, very much so. Thank you." As he is awaiting his food, we begin talking about this shelter. He begins to tell me that this shelter was built back during the time when the great ancestors would hide out from their enemies. "We have been adding to it ever since. That is why it looks like a city beneath the surface of the Earth. As soon as I have finished my breakfast, I will be more than happy to show you around. It's a nice place to see."

"I would like to see this place, sir." So he began to take me around to all the different rooms and explain which rooms and parts were built by his great ancestors. "Sir, I must say, this place is unlike any place I have ever see in my life."

"Well, thank you. Now, these rooms here were built by my grandfather and father when he was growing up back in the late 1800s and early 1900s. You can see the crown molding is made of gold, inlaid by diamonds and rubies which were all hand-carved by my grandfather, the floor being laid-out in pearls and marble."

As we continue to go from room to room, I notice, on several walls, that there are encrusted sculptures of beautiful artwork hand-carved into the walls with diamonds representing the eyes, pearls signifying their smiles, red rubies representing rose-colored lips, cheeks as a pink colored marble, hair as a black onyx, draped slightly over sparkling blue diamond eyes which shone like the stars in heaven's midnight sky. "From here on out," he says, "you will see the hallway to be laid out in yellow gold, inlaid with marble, pearls, and rubies, with their names engraved by hand-cut diamonds."

As we continue our tour of this lovely shelter beneath the earth, we come upon this one room which has a statue of a goddess made of brass. Her face was unlike any other beauty, I have laid my eyes upon. As I stand here, admiring this beautiful statue representing a goddess, he begins to tell me a story that has been told through the generation about who this statue represents. He said she was one of the most beautiful wildflowers who could hypnotize a man just by considering his eyes, which could bring him to his knees. I find myself beginning to softly gaze into her beautiful eyes which sparkle like diamonds with onyx inlaid as he begins to describe her features to me. The shapes of her body, her breasts extending outward like small mountains, and upon those small mountains, a beautiful bronze hilltop. Her hips were curved like a new handcrafted saddle. Her legs were like unto spurs extending from the saddle, and from between those beautiful spurs laid a lovely valley, and from within it flowed a crystal clear stream which carried the needed nutrients to quince one's love for the renewal of the spirit of life to replenish Mother Earth.

"Sir, this place is simply extraordinary, but I must say, with all her beauty, she still cannot even come close to describing my love for her, which I hold so dear within my own heart. If I sowned all of this, I would simply give it all up for love such as hers. To be able to hold such a beautiful sweet angel of a lady as her, who is with me on this journey, in search of a way out of this desert. Just where am I to go next? I don't know where this journey is going to take me next in my life, but I can only hope and pray it will be as far away from this desert. Oh, I can only dream of the day when I'm able to pull her close into my chest and caress her cheek next to mine as I whisper these sweet words into her ears. I do know my sweet love from within my own broken heart. I can't make this world, in which you live, a perfect place for us. I can only try my very best to make it a lovely place for you as we live together under our father's guidance, if you will let me. Only if you can find, from within your own heart, how to let your sweet love flow up onto me like the rains flowing from Heaven. I can only dream of having a sweet angel of a lady such as you to have as my one and only true love, as we both live together under the canopy of heaven."

He looks over at me and says, "My friend, I know just what you are saying, for I also would do just the same. If I could have my one true love back, to hold until the day our Lord comes back for us. There is not a day that goes by that I don't miss her. Just by looking in to her innocent sparkling baby-blue eyes, all my troubles seem to go down with the sun as it went down over the ocean. All I have of her now is nothing but sweet lovely memories of us taking the boys down to the ocean, and as they played in the sand, we would just hold each other and look up into heaven and just talk about our dreams for our family.

Oh, how I do miss those times with her."

"Sir, may I ask you something?"

He says, "Sure, son. What's on your mind?"

"Just how long were you two married?"

"Oh," he says, "Now that's a good question. Let me see here. We got married when I was seventeen years old, and now I'm going to be seventy-eight years old. Now, you do the math and you tell me."

I blurted out, "Whatever do you mean? I do the math and tell you?"

He smiled. "Just do the math, son. Do you know how to add and subtract?

"Well, yes, I do." I come up with sixty-one years.

He said, "Okay then. That is how long we have been together."

I was perplexed and said, "Okay, now you have got me. I don't understand this. You told me that she had passed away some years back, so how could you have been together for sixty-one years?"

"What do you not understand?" he asked.

"How you can say you have been married sixty-one years?"

"Well, son. Once you have found your own one true love in life, there is no other that can take its place."

I ask him, "Have you ever looked for a new love?"

He replied, "Yes, I have dated some other women since she has gone on to be with our Heavenly Father, but I have found none who could even began to come close to my first true love, who my God had given unto me in this journey of life."

"I must agree with you on that, sir, for my first true love must have been only just a dream from which I have now awoken."

He looks at me with a stunned look on his face and asked, "Just what ever do you mean, only just a dream?"

I replied, "Sir, I see it like this. If she was my only one true love, she would not have walked out for someone who she now believes to be her true love."

"Oh," he says. "Sorry. Did not know that she betrayed your love for her in the way that she did."

"Well, sir, to be truthful with you, I felt she didn't love me from the beginning of the marriage, for if she did truly love me like she had said she did in the beginning, well, I don't think she would have not walked out to be with another whatever."

"Son, I'm not sure just what to say about all that took place with her and whatever, but I will say this: just know God is always with you as he has me, for I know he is a great friend."

I replied, "Thank you, sir."

Yes, I shall continue to look unto my Lord for his guidance in all the ways I shall go in life, for He has never let me down. As we continue to walk, I become somewhat hungry and ask him, "Does this place have a nice restaurant?"

He asks, "Just what would you like to eat, son?"

"Oh, I know just what I would love to have, but I know that is not possible."

He turns and looks at me and asks, "What is not possible?"

"I would love to have some of my mom's cooking right now."

He looks at me and says, "Son, I also would love some of my wife's good home-cooked food, but like you said, that is not at all possible. So let's just go on down the hallway. About half a mile away, there is a little restaurant. They do have very good food there." So we get to the restaurant. I tell him to just get me whatever he gets to eat. As we are eating, we talk about going up to see just what kind of damage the storm did to the town.

As we are talking about doing this, up walks someone he knows and he also asks, "Have you been out to see the town?"

"No, we were just talking about doing just that, but I'm now thinking we may need to wait until tomorrow before we go."

"Well, okay," he replied. "Just let me know what time you plan on going up. I would like to go with you."

"Okay, we will let you know when we go."

We start back, I begin to tell him of a time when I was growing up. It was during the time my mom had started dating this man who would later become my new stepdad. I don't know if you recall me tell you about him or not. He is the one who died in the vehicle accident. Well, we went over to his place. He has some hens and one had bites. I asked him if I could have one of the little bites. He said, "Sure, son. If you can catch one, you can have one." So I go out and try to catch one, but what this five-year old boy didn't know was that the mother hen would turn on me. She started flapping her wings and chasing after me all the way across the yard. I ran as hard as I could up to the porch to get away from her. Well, needless to say, I did not get a little yellow bite. As I was telling him this, he started to laugh.

He asked, "Did you not know a mother would protect her little ones as your mother would you?"

"Well no, sir," I replied. "I was just five and didn't know any better." We start to make our way back. We pass one of the most attractive ladies, I have seen outside of the one that is with me. I asked him if he knew her.

"No, I don't think so," he replied.

I responded, "Well, she is one lovely looking lady that I would love to meet."

He asked, "What about the lady that is with you now? I thought she is the one you wanted?"

All I could said was, "I now don't think she will be going on from here with me, for she seems to have her sights set on your friend's son. I just need to forget about her and begin to look elsewhere for my beloved help-mate. I don't know where I may find her. I do know one thing, and that, my friend, is this. If I'm not looking, I'm not going to find her."

Well, we are back and I'm one tired person. I go to my room to read from the book of Ruth.

BOOK ABOUT RUTH

Here, I begin to think, I have find true integrity of a godly woman, who is willing to put one's family first and foremost. Ruth was the daughter-in-law of Elimelech and Naomi. Elimelech died, leaving Naomi with her two sons and their wives. The names of their sons were Mahlon and Chi lion. They took wives of the country of Moab. The names of their wives were Orpah and Ruth. They lived in the land for ten years. Then Mahlon and Chi lion died also, leaving their wives with Naomi. Naomi tried her best to talk the women into going back to their people, but Ruth would not do so. She was bound and determined to go with Naomi to take care of her in her old age.

> And Naomi had a kinsman of her husband's, a mighty man of wealth, of the family of Elimelech, and his name was Boaz. And Ruth the Moabitess said unto Naomi, Let me now go to the field, and glean ears of corn after him in whose sight I shall find grace. And she said unto her, Go, my daughter. (Ruth 2:1–3, KJV)
> Wash thyself therefore, and anoint thee, and put thy raiment upon thee, and get thee down to the floor: but make not thyself known unto the man,

until he shall have done eating and drinking. And it shall be, when he lieth down, that thou shalt mark the place where he shall lie, and thou shalt go in, and uncover his feet, and lay thee down, and he will tell thee what thou shalt do. And she said unto her, All that thou sayest unto me I will do. And she went down unto the floor, and did according to all that her mother in law bade her. (Ruth 3:3–6, KJV)

As I continue to read in the book of Ruth. I find her to be a woman of great integrity and one who kept her faith in God who later becomes a great ancestor to our Lord, Jesus Christ, who sacrificed His life upon an old rugged cross for my sins.

DAYS AFTER
THE STORM

I get up and go in to the kitchen where they are sitting. I pour myself a cup of coffee and sit down with them at the table. We begin to talk about going out to see just what kind of damage has been done to the town. I've got to say, as we make our way around the town, it is in good condition for the most part. Some of the stores had a great bit of damage.

As we make our way down to the dock, I find myself heartbroken, for the only way I was to leave this desert had been washed ashore by the storm. I look at the captain, and he looks at me and says, "My friend, it's looking like we're going to be here for some time to come. We must find some way to dig a channel around the ship deep enough to allow water to get beneath it for it to be able to float back out in to the ocean."

After he has said this, I look over at the older gentleman, who said he owned the ship, and ask if he knew where we might find a backhoe to dig this deep channel. He replies, "I think there is one over in the next town, but I don't know just how we are going to get it here."

I ask him, "If they do have one, do you think they would let us borrower it?"

The captain asks me, "Do you know how to operate one?"

I look at him and say, "I can do what ever I set my mind to do. I do believe, if need be, I could dig the channel with a shovel."

He looks at me and says, "If we can't get a backhoe here, you might be doing just that." We make our way back to the shelter to let everyone know that the town is in good condition and they can return to their homes. As we do, I see this lady from the day before and she looks just as beautiful as she did yesterday. Her eyes sparkle like a blue diamond with onyx inlaid within them. Her beautiful smile shines brighter than pearls. Her lips are as red roses and feel as soft petals when ours met for the first time. They taste as sweet as honey when ours touch. Her cheeks shine as pink marble and feels like soft silk as we softly caressed each other. Her long, silky autumn hair flows like the wind as she sashayed across the open plains of this desert and into a valley wherein lies a beautiful meadow from whence flows the steam of life.

I look back over at the gentleman who owns the motorcycle shop and ask if I could borrow one of his bikes to go into the next town tomorrow to see if they have a backhoe that we could borrow to dig this channel. He replies, "Yes, you may, my friend, but this time, I'm going with you. I would like to check on someone I knew that live there. I have not seen her in about thirty years or more."

"Oh," I replied. "Is she one of the wildflowers that you dated after your wife passed away?"

He replied, "No, son. She was the one who I loved before I had met my wife. I was about ten years older than her. Her family would not approve of us being together because I was older than her. That was long before I got married to the loveliest wildflower that I ever laid eyes on."

"May I ask you, sir, do you know if she ever got married?"

He looks over at me and said, "I don't know if she ever did or not. I have thought about her a lot since my wife had passed away. But not knowing if she did or not, I never try to get back in touch with her after I left. But now, I find myself wanting to see her one more time before I leave this life journey. I'm seventy-eight, and my life here is almost over. I would love to tell her that I have often thought of her through the years. I cannot forget how her beautiful, innocent, sweet face looks when she smiles. Her smile alone gave my life new meaning. If only she knew how her beautiful innocent smile alone could give one's fading heart the breath of new life. I can only hope in my prayers, when I leave this journey of life, that the one whom is standing by my side will share their beautiful smile. Letting me know in my heart, by their smile alone, that there is a life forevermore awaiting me in their Father's Kingdom."

"Sir," I replied. "That is lovely. I would love to find, with in my own heart, words like those and be able to say them to the wildflower that is with me here in this desert. I don't think, even if I could find with in my own heart words like those, it would do me any good. For it appears that she has fallen head over heels in love with you friend's son."

Well," he said, "son, I'm very sorry you feel that way. Maybe, by the time you get to where you are going, you will have find, in your heart, the words to say to the one you feel is to be your true love and win her heart."

"Thank you, sir. I know one day I will find my true love somewhere out in this big old world. I shall keep on looking for her, but just where, I don't know."

Would you like a cup of coffee?"

"No, sir. Thank you. I think I'll go on to bed. See you tomorrow."

"Okay, son. See you then. Oh, and don't forget, we are to leave early in the morning. We are to go over to the next town and see if they have a backhoe."

"Got it." I go back to my room and pick up where I had stopped in the book of Ruth.

> So Boaz took Ruth, and she was his wife: and when he went in unto her, the Lord gave her conception, and she bare a son. And the women said unto Naomi, Blessed be the Lord, which hath not left thee this day without a kinsman, that his name may be famous in Israel. And he shall be unto thee a restorer of thy life, and a nourisher of thine old age: for thy daughter in law, which loveth thee, which is better to thee than seven sons, hath born him. And Naomi took the

child, and laid it in her bosom, and became nurse
unto it. (Ruth 4:13–16, KJV)

Now a new day is upon us and we are to go into the next town
and try to find a backhoe to dig with. And he would like to check
on his old friend, and I myself would like to see if the flower shop is
still open. I would like to find something there to give to the lovely
wildflower that was once with me on this journey. I know that the
first yellow and red rose did not work out the way I was hoping they
would. But this one will be the one that will say farewell to the loveliest woman I have had the pleasure of being around.

As he is driving to the next town, we talk about how deep the
channel needs to be for the ship to float back into the ocean. I ask him
if he knows just where in this town we need to go to find this backhoe
that we are in so much need of. He replies, "Son, all I can tell you is
that we're going to ask someone, because I have not a clue."

I then ask him, "Do you know just where you first love lives?"

He did reply, "What is with all these questions? Can't you see
I'm trying to drive?"

"Well, I'm sorry. Didn't mean to distract you, you old grouch."

"Oh, what did you just call me?"

"Oh, not a thing, sir. Just keep your eyes on the road."

"Oh okay, son. I just have a lot on my mind right now, for I'm
looking forward to seeing her again. It has been forty years or more
since I last saw her. I'm hoping she will remember me. I did love her
with all my heart. I remember her beautiful smile and how it made me
feel when we were together. When I considered her baby-brown eyes,
they had a sparkle like the stars in the midnight skies. She just has a
way about her that made my heart feel like it was going to beat right
through my chest. Her lips shine pink as a flame of fire. When her lips
first touched mine, man, I tell you. Her kiss melted me to my knees.
I knew right then she was the one for me, but her dad didn't think so.

"The day that I had to leave her behind was the hardest day of in
my life. Well, at the time it was, until the day came that my true love
passed away."

As we come in to the town, we stop at this story and asked the
cashier if he knew where we could find a backhoe. He replied, "Sir, you

go down to the first stop light and take a left. About a half a mile or so, you will find one there. That, if they haven't been rented out by now."

"My friend here would like to ask you a question, if you don't mind him asking."

"Sure, I don't mind."

"My question is, sir, do you know if this lady still lives here in this town?"

He replies, "Yes, sir. She still lives here."

"Do you know where she is living?"

"Yes, sir. You go on past the first stoplight, you will come to a four-way stop. You take a right. The best I remember, she lives on the left, about three houses down from the stop sign."

"Thank you, sir, for your help."

"Oh, no problem. Glad I could help. Hope you find what you are looking for."

"Well," I ask, "do you want to go see if we can find the backhoe first or do you want to see her first?"

"Well," he says, "I would like to see her first, but I think we need to find a backhoe first."

I'm thinking the same thing, but I was not going to say anything. So we head out to find the backhoe shop first. When we get there, all we see on the yard are track hoes. We look at each other and ask, "How are we getting this back?" We go in and I ask the owner if he had any more backhoes for rent.

He looks at me and says, "Sir, all my backhoes are all out cleaning up from the storm that came through two days ago. Now I do have the track hoes outside that I can rent you if you'd like to use one of them."

"Yes, sir. I'm in much need of one, but there's this one problem, sir. I have no way of getting it back to where I'm needing it. All we have is a small truck with a small trailer. I know it will not haul a big track hoe."

"Oh," he says, "I see. Well, today is your lucky day, my friend. It just so happens I also have a truck and trailer that I can rent you. Are you interested in renting all three for one low price?"

"Well, just how low of a price are you asking, sir?" I ask.

"Well," he asks, "just how long are you gentlemen going to need it?"

The gentleman who owns the motorcycle shop replied, "Sir, right now, we can't say for sure, for we must dig a channel around the supply ship that got pushed a shore by the storm."

"Oh, I'm sorry to hear this. Maybe I can rent it to you for three hundred dollars a week, that's if you can put a down payment of a thousand dollars."

"Did he just say a thousand dollars?" my friend asks me.

"Yes, he said a thousand dollars."

"Oh, okay. That's what I thought I heard him say."

I then reply to the owner, "We will take all three and we can pick them up."

"Show me your thousand dollars and you can come back in two hours and pick it up."

"Okay, I'm going to need a receipt showing where we paid you the thousand dollars as a down payment."

"Okay, sir. Here's your receipt, and like I said, you can pick it up in two hours."

"Thank you. We will be back." We head out to find the lady he is looking for. We get to the place we thought she lived, only to find out she had moved two blocks down the road.

He asked the man if he knew just what house she was living in now. "Sir, I think she is in the first house on the right."

So we go two blocks down the road and he sees her on the front porch. He looks at me with a big smile on his face and says, "Son, she looks just as beautiful today as she did when I first met her forty-something years ago."

We get out and walk up the porch. She asks, "Can I be some help to you both?" He said her name, she looked at him, and a big grin came up on her face. I thought she was going to jump off the porch into his arms when she realized who he was. She says, "Come on up and have a seat here with me." They started talking about the good old days, back when they first started dating. He asked her if she ever got married. "Yes, I did," she replied. "I got married about five years after you left. e have two grown sons and one daughter. Did you ever marry? she asked.

He replies, "Yes, I did, and we also have two grown sons, but she passed away when she was carrying our third child."

"Oh, I'm so sorry to hear that, my old friend. My husband passed away six years ago, and I have been here all alone ever since."

He asked, "What about your two sons? Do they ever come to visit you?"

"Yes, they come from time to time, but it is not the same as having someone here with me all the time." She asks, "Do your sons ever visit you?"

"Yes, they live just a short piece from my motorcycle shop. They are in and out all the time, helping me with everything around the shop. One's running the shop I have across town." I'm looking at the time, and it has been an hour and half now and we need to be on our way back to pick up the track hoe. He sees me looking at the time and says, "Yes, son. I know we need to be going."

"May I suggest something to you?"

"What's on your mind?" he asks.?

"Well, sir. You take me to pick up the track hoe, then you could come back and spend more time with her."

"Now, son," he says, "that is the best idea you have had in a long time, that is, if it's okay with her."

She replies, "I would love for you to come back."

"Okay, let's get going son." He looks at her and says, "I'll be back as fast as I can, little lady." I'm thinking how he is seventy-eight and she is sixty-eight. What he had said about their first kiss and how it melted him to his knees. I'm thinking if she gives him a kiss like that, it might melt more than his knees, it might just kill him this time. As we start our way back to pick up the truck and track-hoe, he begins to tell me that he's going to ask her to marry him and move-back home to the town in which he lives.

"Well, sir. If she accepts your proposal, I do wish you both a long and happy life together." I'm thinking to myself, *This has been one journey, I would like to forget sooner than later, but only time will tell.*

Oh, Lord, hear my heart's cry, for I'm praying for your forgiveness for my failures and imperfection. Oh, Lord, help me to find within my own soul to forgive my brothers and sisters, as you have forgiven me. If they could only realize or even begin to understand just how the words that they sometimes say can cut someone's soul so deep that it leaves a scar on one's heart, making it hard to recover. Oh, Lord, I only ask of you to help them find, within their own hearts, the will to forgive others for their failures and imperfections as well. For one can not help how you have molded them to be. (Oh, hold on now, for someone has just suggested that he is asking for sympathy.) No, he is only asking for understanding for his failures and imperfections. I ask of you, have you forgotten that you are not to pass judgement and think that you are better than he is? May I ask of you, do you consider yourself to be a born-again Christian, and do you think your actions fall in line with God's teaching? If so, why would you say that one would be asking for sympathy? Is that the way a born-again Christian is to conduct one's self? Being born of the spirit of God, have you forgotten that, in God's eyes, you are both created equally? In God's eyes, there is no respect of persons. He has not one person which he cannot use at his own will. For you both are created in His own image. Let's go look in the living words of Matthew and see just what is said about judging and prejudging someone for their imperfection.

> Judge not, that ye be not judged. For with what judgment ye judge, ye shall be judged: and with what measure ye mete, it shall be measured to you again. And why beholdest thou the mote that is in thy brother's eye, but considerest not the beam that is in thine own eye? Or how wilt thou say to thy brother, Let me pull out the mote out of thine eye, and, behold, a beam is in thine own eye? Thou hypocrite, first cast out the beam out of thine own eye, and then shalt thou see clearly to cast out the mote out of thy brother's eye. (Matthew 7:1–5, KJV)

Now, with this being read from Matthew, and the question being asked of you. Do you still think and feel that your actions are in line with God's teaching? Do you still not understand that, by looking down on someone for their imperfections, it does not help them or you? You may not realize it, but you just placed a snare for thy brother to fall into and one for yourself. You may not realize this, but it only took one sin for God to kick Lucifer and a third of his angels out of His Kingdom. Do you know just what sin Lucifer committed for God to kick him out of his kingdom? I would like to share a scripture or two from King James Bible.

> For thou hast said in thine heart, I will ascend into heaven, I will exalt my throne above the stars of God: I will sit also upon the mount of the congregation, in the sides of the north: I will ascend above the heights of the clouds, I will be like the most High. (Isaiah 14:13–14, KJV)

So I say unto you, just stop and put some thought into what you going to say to someone before you do. Your choice of words could make a big impact on that person's life. Now, you may think I'm judging you, but no, that is just the opposite. What I just did is judge the fruit of your actions towards your fellow man or woman, for I do believe that you can tell a born-again Christian by the fruit which they bear, the fruit being one's actions and choosing of one's words. Now, shall we take a closer consideration of the words of Matthew 7 and see just what he says to us.

> Beware of false prophets, which come to you in sheep's clothing, but inwardly they are ravening wolves. Ye shall know them by their fruits. Do men gather grapes of thorns, or figs of thistles? Even so every good tree bringeth forth good fruit, but a corrupt tree bringeth forth evil fruit. A good tree cannot bring forth evil fruit, neither can a corrupt tree bring forth good fruit. Every tree that bringeth not forth good fruit is hewn down, and cast into the fire. Wherefore by their fruits ye shall know them. (Matthew 7:15–20, KJV)

Now, may I ask, do you think by your actions and choice of words, that you are bringing forth good fruits? Now, may we go to the words of Luke and see what is said in chapter 6?

> For a good tree bringeth not forth corrupt fruit, neither doth a corrupt tree bring forth good fruit. For every tree is known by his own fruit. For of thorns men do not gather figs, nor of a bramble bush gather they grapes. A good man out of the good treasure of his heart bringeth forth that which is good, and an evil man out of the evil treasure of his heart bringeth forth that which is evil: for of the abundance of the heart his mouth speaketh. (Luke 6:43–45, KJV)

ONE'S ACTIONS

Now, I'm not trying to say to you here, in any way, that you are not a Christian, for that is not for me to judge. But what I am trying to say is that people need to check their actions and choice of words and the way in which they use them before each other. Now I know, with in my own heart, that I'm going to be looked down on for what I am going to say next. There are people in this world, just like the ones back in the days of Moses. When things were going the way they wanted them to go, it was all okay, but when things didn't go so well, what did they all do? Well, they turn their backs on God, just like so many people are doing today. People look to some other gods for their answers, instead of doing what our true God has asked of them and that is to repent of their sins and turn from their iniquity. You say that this is a Christian nation, one that puts God first in their lives. May I ask, why is it so often people are looking down on other religions for the way in which they believe? If only the people were to put as much emphasis on their religion as others do, and practice their true faith in which they say is to the living God. The people have forgotten just what a born-again Christian is about. No, I'm not saying that all religions are of the true born-again Christian faith. I would like to just ask you something here, if I may. Are you doing what is required of you as a born-again Christian? Have you forgotten how one as a born-again Christian should conduct them selves around others? I am sorry to say, yes, and the truth hurts. Why am I saying this, you ask? Well, take a long, good look around you at what is going on in this world in which we live in today. People who proclaim to be born-again Christians have gotten so far out of line with the true teaching of God's word, and that, within itself, is a crying shame. People ask, "Why is there so much killing going on in this world?" or, "Why is there so much adultery being committed? Why is my child behaving the way they are? Why did my son or daughter become a homosexual?" Well, I ask you once again, are you doing your part as a born-again Christian? Are you teaching them to be walking in line with the word of God? Oh, so you send them to school and take them to church every Sunday. Do you not realize that there are so many people who are teaching in schools today, who do not believe in God? Who have not come to accept Jesus as their personal savior? Why am I saying this? Well, look at some of the ones that say there is no God who are teaching your child. Oh, I see what you are saying here, is that we are putting our responsibility as a parent off on someone else to teach our child how to walk in line with Gods teaching. When the Christians of this nation has let the ungodly non-believing, people deceive you to the port that you have let them take away your rights as a Christian. Don't deceived yourself by thinking that everyone who is teaching your children, has their best interest at heart: for it could be someone who may not believe in God who is teaching your child. Now let's look in the living word of God, on how one should be teaching their children.

> By humility and the fear of the Lord are riches, and honour, and life. Thorns and snares are in the way of the froward: he that doth keep his soul shall be far from them. Train up a child in the way he should go: and when he is old, he will not depart from it. The rich ruleth over the poor, and the borrower is servant to the lender. He that soweth iniquity shall reap vanity: and the rod of his anger shall fail. (Proverbs 22:4–8, KJV)

The rod and reproof give wisdom: but a child left to himself bringeth his mother to shame. When the wicked are multiplied, transgression increaseth: but the righteous shall see their fall. Correct thy son, and he shall give thee rest, yea, he shall give delight unto thy soul. (Proverbs 29:15–17, KJV)

UNGRATEFUL AND SELFISH NATION

Ungrateful and selfish nation. We as a Born-Again Christian Nation have somehow, along the way, let our wants come before our needs. I know, from being of the flesh, that that is the easiest thing to do. We see things that we think we need, but in reality, it's this flesh telling you that you've got have this. So we go and borrow the money to buy it. Now that you have taken on more than you can handle, one may ask, "What do you mean more than I can handle?" Well, it's like this, you now have more of your time taken away. Now you must work longer hours to pay the money back to the lender. You now have lost time to put more embassy on teaching your children in the way they should be living for God. Just look up the first scripture. We must turn back to our God and ask for his forgiveness and repent of our own self-righteousness. We also need to get our priorities in line with God's word. We have become such an ungrateful and selfish nation. How can you say this? Just why would someone say that this is an ungrateful and selfish world in which we live? Just take a good look around you, at all the ungodly acts that people are committing in this world.

If you can't see what is right before your eyes. They have become disrespectful. A disgrace to themselves and others around them by their only conduct, through their ungodly actions, and what they participate in. All the adultery, idolatry, immorality, and homosexuality that is occurring in this would. They have become likened unto thieves, murderers, and egotistical self-righteous people. You say you are a born-again Christian. Well, that's not for me to judge. What I am seeing is the fruit which you bear for every word which spews out of your mouth being good or filled with every vulgar language which any one can think of under the canopy of Heaven. Do you not know or understand that by you doing this, you are telling your brother and sister and the rest of the world that you don't have any self-respect or self-remorse for the word of God whom you have said has forgiven you for your sins? How, then, can you, as a born-again Christian, expect to bring someone who has not yet come to know and accept Jesus as their personal savior when you show them only the iniquity of your actions which do not align with the true teaching of God's word? If you are not seeing all this taking place in this world today, well, you just may need to get back to living by the true way of God's words.

For those of you who have shown disrespect for the American flag and the National Anthem. Do you not understand the true meaning of what they represent? By your only cohesive acts, you are showing disrespect to all of those who paid the ultimate price on the battlefield. In John 15: 13, it says, "Greater love has no one than this, that someone lay down his life for his friends." By you burning, urinating on, trampling on, etc. you are saying to your brother and sister that you don't have any remorse or respect for their blood that they gave up for your freedom. For the words have been said, where much is given, much is required. How much more can one give than to lay their lives down for self-righteous ungrateful, selfish, unrighteous, individuals than for those who are living in the world today. You only kneel in reverence to the blood that Jesus shed that day upon the cross for your salvation. You stand for those who have sacrificed their lives on the battlefield for the freedom which you have. You have become just like those who your brothers and sisters have fought against to defend your freedom. For those who uphold you in doing such an ungodly and selfish act, there is no noble cause. For you to disrespect their brothers and sisters in such a way that you have. For thy brothers and sisters blood that they shed on the battlefield, it's for your freedom, not your salvation, so why would you kneel? You have brought disgrace upon the blood of Jesus and yourself. There is no other greater cause for you to kneel other than the blood of Jesus Christ, for his life, which he gave up so freely. If it came down to you being called upon to defend your only freedom, you would more likely run the other way. You do not have the backbone in you to stand up and do what is right. Do you not know or understand what the stripes on the American flag represent? The red stripe represent the blood of the brothers and sisters who have shed for your freedom. The white signifies the purity and innocence of those who have shed their blood for the freedom which you now take for granted. If you did not, you would not do the things you do. You are a very fortunate person to have the choice to do as you have.

Let's just go back once more to the living word of God, to see what it must say about the way in which the people of this world are living. What do you mean how the people are living? Do you not know in God's eyes that it is an abomination to be living the way some are in this world today? There are people who are living in this country today, just like they did in the days of Sodom. Well, to start out with, it's all about me, me, me. Then there is this word called "racist" that everyone seems to love to use to their advantage, politically correct speaking as not to hurt someone fragile feelings, murder, homosexuality, idolatry, and the list just keeps growing. Do you think that God is pleased with a country as this that is upholding these kinds of behaviors and actions? Now, looking back to the words of God. For those who do believe in God, and for the ones who don't. For these are his words unto the people as a born-again Christian through His son, Jesus. Now, in the book of Genesis 19, you well find just what it says about all the above acts in which people are partaking in. For there are some men and women who are standing behind the pulpits of some churches who partake in such acts and uphold such acts. Be ye not deceived by them. For they believe that it is okay for someone to commit such acts so as not to offend their fragile feelings.

> I speak to your shame. Is it so, that there is not a wise man among you? no, not one that shall be able to judge between his brethren? But brother goeth to law with brother, and that before the unbelievers. Now therefore there is utterly a fault among you, because ye go to law one with another. Why do ye not rather take wrong? why do ye not rather suffer yourselves to be defrauded? Nay, ye do wrong, and defraud, and that your brethren. Know ye not that the unrighteous shall not inherit the kingdom of God? Be not deceived: neither fornicators, nor idolaters, nor adulterers, nor effeminate, nor abusers of themselves with mankind, Nor thieves, nor covetous, nor drunkards, nor revilers, nor extortioners, shall inherit the kingdom of God. And such were some of you: but ye are washed, but ye are sanctified, but ye are justified in the name of the Lord Jesus, and by the Spirit of our God. (1 Corinthians 6:5–11, KJV)

Just go look in the book of 1 Timothy 1:10 and see what Paul wrote to Timothy concerning such acts. Leviticus 18 in the King James Bible, starting with verse one. You need to read this one for yourself. Reading from the book of Romans 1:26–32 has this to say about such acts.

> For this cause God gave them up unto vile affections: for even their women did change the natural use into that which is against nature: And likewise also the men, leaving the natural use of the woman, burned in their lust one toward another, men with men working that which is unseemly, and receiving in themselves that recompence of their error which was meet. And even as they did not like to retain God in their knowledge, God gave them over to a reprobate

mind, to do those things which are not convenient, Being filled with all unrighteousness, fornication, wickedness, covetousness, maliciousness, full of envy, murder, debate, deceit, malignity, whisperers, Backbiters, haters of God, despiteful, proud, boasters, inventors of evil things, disobedient to parents, Without understanding, covenantbreakers, without natural affection, implacable, unmerciful: Who knowing the judgment of God, that they which commit such things are worthy of death, not only do the same, but have pleasure in them that do them. (Romans 1:26–32, KJV)

Looking in the book of Matthew 10 as to what Jesus had to say to His disciples about such ungodly acts.

And whosoever shall not receive you, nor hear your words, when ye depart out of that house or city, shake off the dust of your feet. Verily I say unto you, It shall be more tolerable for the land of Sodom and Gomorrha in the day of judgment, than for that city. (Matthew 10:14–15, KJV)

THE DOUBLE-EDGED SWORD

For I ask you this, does this not sound like the nation in which you live in today has become? Do you not understand what God did to the land of Sodom and Gomorrah? He destroyed that land and the people in it with brimstone and fire for the very same reasons. The people who are living in this country today are now committing the same ungodly acts as they did in the days of Sodom and Gomorrah. Have you forgetter the way in which you are to be living for God? I will say this, one's actions alone speak loud and clear as for who you put your faith.

I have asked this one question repeatedly. Why have the children of this generation become so disrespectful and ungrateful? The one and only answer I get is this. We want them to have more than what we had when we were growing up. We therefore give them everything they want and not their one true need. With this being the only answer I get. Then I would like to ask, what are you doing about this? Just what would you say their needs are? Let me also ask, what did your parents say to you when you saw something that you thought you needed? If your parents were like most parents when I was growing up, they would have said you don't need that boy or girl. If you got your little fragile feelings hurt and became disrespectful with them, they didn't take away your cellphone, TV, computer,

Gameboy, Xbox, etc. Do you think by taking something like this away from someone that it is teaching them the true meaning of one's self-respect and self-discipline? No, not back in the days when I was growing up. You got a rod put to your backside. What does God's word say about the discipline of a child?

> He that spareth his rod hateth his son: but he that loveth him chasteneth him betimes. (Proverbs 13:24, KJV)

> Remove not the old landmark, and enter not into the fiels of the fatherless: For their redeemer is mighty, he shall plead their cause with thee. Apply thine heart unto in-struction, and thine ears to the words of knowledge. Withhold not correction from the child: for if thou beatest him with the rod, he shall not die. Thou shalt beat him with the rod, and shalt deliver his soul from hell. (Proverbs 23:10–14, KJV)

May I reflect to my first writing, where I said my step-dad whooped me once. I must say, he did not spare the rod that day, and to this day, I have a much greater respect for the words of their living God. He put the fear of God in me by putting my needs first and not my wants. The people have forgotten how to teach their children the difference between their needs and their wants by sparing them the rod from time to time. It has gotten so far out of control that it has become shameful and disgraceful for a nation who says that it's a Christian nation. You can and may say this is a Christian nation, but a Christian nation that has turned their backs on God, just as they did when Moses lead God's people out of Egypt. Have you ever heard this before? What? My mind is going ninety to nothing. Whatever do you mean ninety to nothing? Well it's like this. There is so much going through my mind right now that I can't keep it all together and get it to come out right. I must give this old brain a rest for now. Hopefully, you have enjoyed what you have read so far. But before I go, I would like to share one last thought with you. For this just came to mind, way back when Jesus was being crucified for our sins on that ol' cross. Do you recall what He said that day when He shed his blood while it ran down his side? He said, "Father, forgive them for they know not what they do." Goodnight, and may God have mercy upon you.

Now we are back to where I am to pick up the truck and track hoe. I go in and ask for the keys. The owner tells me that he needs to show me something about the track hoe. So we go out to where he has them set up. He tells me the hydraulic tank is low and that I needed to add some before operating the system. I ask, "Do you not have any?"

"No, sir," he replies. "I'm all out because of the storm, I had to put all we had in the backhoes to get them up and running for the cleanup here."

"Okay, sir. I just hope they have some back where I'm going. If not, I don't know what we are going to do next." Well, I make it back with the track hoe, only to find out from the captain that we've got to wait until tomorrow before I can start digging the channel around the ship. I ask, "Why is this, captain?" He tells me that, while I was gone to find a backhoe or track hoe, he called back for a tugboat to come and assist in getting the ship pulled out in to the ocean, and they would be here in about two days or so. "Oh, okay," I replied. "That is great. They will be able to help pull the ship back out into the ocean. Now, in the meantime, I need to find some hydraulic fluid for the track hoe."

He asks, "Where is the gentleman who went with you to get the track hoe?"

I tell him, "He is back with his first love and he said that he was going to ask her to marry him and move back here and live out the rest of their lives together as one."

"Oh, I see," he says. "She must be one of a kind."

"Yes, sir, she is a beautiful lady."

He asks, "Did you find what you were looking for?"

"No, sir. I didn't have the time to go looking around the town. I was more worried about finding a track hoe to work with." We get everything set up to start the work tomorrow. I go back to the shop for the rest of the day and find her there.

She asks, "How are you today?"

"I'm okay, thanks for asking. How about you?"

"Oh, I'm great," she says. "Would you like something to eat or drink? I would be more than happy to fix it for you."

"That would be very nice of you, thanks. I could user something to eat. It has been a long day." While she prepares the meal, I go into the other room and sit down and fall asleep.

The owner of the shop comes in and wakes me up, and begins to tell me that he got married. I look at him and ask, "What did you just say?"

He says, "She said yes, so, we got married, making me the happiest man once again to ever live under the canopy of heaven. Will you go with me tomorrow and help move her things?"

"Well, I guess I can. I need to go back there myself and look for something."

She comes in about the time I'm telling him this, and says, "The meal is ready, if you'd like to eat now."

"Thank you," I reply. "We'll be in shortly, beautiful."

She looks at me with her lovely smile and says, "You're welcome." As we are eating, I tell him what the captain told me. He had called back on his radio asking for assistance from a tub boat, and they would be here in about two days. She asks, "What is a tub boat?"

He also looks at me. "Yes, just what is a tub boat son?"

"That is a question you need to ask the captain. Thank you for the great meal. I'm going to say good night now and go bed, I hope to see you tomorrow." I go my room and read the words of James 3:8–13.

> But the tongue can no man tame, it is an unruly evil, full of deadly poison. Therewith bless we God, even the Father, and therewith curse we man, which are made after the similitude of God. Out of the same mouth proceedeth blessing and cursing, my brethren, these things ought not so to be. Doth a fountain sends forth at the same place sweet water and bitter? Can the fig tree, my brethren, bear olive berries? Either a vine, figs? So, can no fountain both yield salt water and fresh. Who is a wise man and endued with knowledge among you? Let him shew out of good conversation his works with meekness of wisdom. (James 3:8–13, KJV)

THE NEW WIFE
MOVES IN

"**G**ood morning, sir. I hope you had a good night's sleep. I, for one, did."

"Thanks, son, but I must say I didn't. All I could think about was my new wife. Oh, how I wish she was already here with me. I can hardly wait until she has moved in. You are still going to help me get her things moved today?"

"Yes, sir. I'm going to help you if you need me. Do you still have the trailer hooked up?"

"Yes, I do, son."

"Good, then we can head out as soon as I get a bite to eat and a cup of coffee."

"Son," he says, "you can get something to eat at her house. We need to be going now."

"Well, you are in a big hurry. Can I at least get a cup of coffee?"

"Yes," he replies, "only if you get it to go."

"Oh, thank you, sir. I will do just that." So, I get my coffee, and out the door we go. As we head out to move his wife's things to his place, he begins to tell me about the time he was working for this company that rented out heavy equipment such as bulldozers, backhoes, track hoes and dump trucks. I asked, "How long did you work for this company?"

"Well, I worked there about twenty years. Well, that was up to right after my first wife passed away. Now," he says as the story goes, "the company he was working for hired this kid and put him working with me," he says. "We were out inspecting some equipment after it had been washed by the construction workers who had rented the equipment for a week or two to do some road work. They were out on the wash rack, washing some of the vehicles. When they got done with one, they would come and ask if one of us would look it over. Well, one of the guys came over and asked if I would look at his vehicle, so I go over and look at it and tell him there is still some mud inside the wheel.

"Well, this new kid that was working with me comes over running his mouth, telling me he had already looked at this vehicle. I didn't know just what in the I was talking about right out in front of the customers. He says, 'you just stupid as one can be, for you have no idea what you even talking about. You're just ate-up with stupidity, and I now see why everyone says the things they do about you when you are not around.'

"Some the customers are looking at him. One asks, 'What is his problem, and why is he talking to you in that way?'

"I reply, 'I think he is one of the higher management's nephews, who has always been allowed to have his way in everything and hadn't been taught what respect is.' So, I go over and look at this other vehicle that they wanted me to be looked at. He goes back over to the side and lights up a cigarette. After I had look this other vehicle over, I head back to let the boss know that I had cleared this vehicle. Well, on my way back, the new kid steps up and grabs me by the nape of the neck. Well, I knocked his hand off and told him if he ever did that again, oh what I would do. He was to stay away from me and not say nothing else to me for the rest of the day. I go on over and let the boss know I had cleared one more vehicle."

"Well, may I ask you sir? Did he leave you alone for the rest of the day like you had asked him?"

"Well, to answer your question, son. No, he didn't. You know just how some people are. They like to see how far they can push someone before they go off on them. This kid just had to smart off his mouth once again that day. I'm guessing the boss did not see him grab me earlier this morning out on the wash rack. All he saw and heard was me telling him I didn't want to hear another word from him. He needs to stay away and leave me alone, like I had asked him to do earlier that morning.

"Well, he just kept running his mouth, and I'm telling him once again to go on and mind his own business and leave me alone. I knew what I had been asked to do. Well, as I start to head out, up walks the supervisor and tells me that he is going to start the paperwork on getting me fired because I can't seem to get along with anybody nowadays. 'You had no business getting all up in his face like you did earlier this morning, and you have no right to talk to him the in the way you have.'

"I then reply, 'Sir, with all due respect, what you did not see or know is what had taken place prior to me getting in his face, and that, sir, is the way in which he had talked to me and grabbed me by the nape of the neck for no reason. It's like he's wanting to fight. Now that part, sir, is what you didn't see, and that is the only reason I got in his face and did not beat his face into the ground. If it had been any one else he had done that way, I assure you, they would have beat the life out of him right then and there. All I ask is for him not to talk to me for the rest of the day, and now you are telling me, sir, that I can't get along with anyone and you're going to start the paperwork to have me fired for something he had started.'"

"Well, sir. Did he fire you?"

"No, son. I just got told I needed to be a bigger man even though he was the one who grabbed me by the nape of the neck, for that did not give me the right to get in his face. I'm listening to the supervisor tell me how I need to be the bigger man. I'm thinking, what would he do if I walked up and grabbed him by the nape of the neck? Would he be a bigger man and walk away and let it go as if it never took place? What do you think son?"

"Well, sir. I think he would have fired you right then and there, because he has the power to do so. Now as for yourself, sir, I think you did just what you thought a bigger man should do, and that is to walk away, not beating his face against your fist like most people would have."

"Yes, son. I could have beaten the life out of him, but I didn't."

"Well, sir. It sounds as if you chose to do what you felt was right in your own heart and that was walking away, showing yourself as being the bigger man. Your story, sir, reminds me of what I read last night in James 3:8–13.

What do you mean, son? It reminds you of James 3:13?"

"Well, it's like this, sir. You walked away, showing you as being a wise man and endowed with knowledge. You showed, out of your good conversation, your work with meekness of wisdom by walking away and not escalating the situation to the point of beating his face against your fist. Now, sir, do you think that the new kid showed any knowledge and wisdom in the way he grabbed you by the nape of the neck and continued to push you after you had asked him to leave you alone?"

"Well, no, son. I never thought about it in that way, I guess one could see it as being that way. But I see it as being this in James 2:17–26."

> Even so faith, if it hath not works is dead, being alone. Yea, a man may say, thou hast faith, and I have works: shew me thy faith without thy works, and I will shew thee my faith by my works. Thou believest that there is on God, thou doest well: the devils also believe, and tremble. But wilt thou know, O vain man, that faith without works is dead? Was not Abraham our father justified by works, when he had offered Isaac his son upon the altar? Seest thou how faith wrought with his works, and by works was faith made perfect? And the scripture was fulfilled which saith, Abraham believed God, and it was imputed unto him for righteousness: and he was called the Friend of God. Ye see then how that by works a man is justified, and not by faith only. Likewise, also was not Rahab the harlot justified by works, when she had received the

messengers, and had sent them out another way?
For as the body without the spirit is dead, so faith
without works is dead also. (James 2:17–26, KJV)

He then says, "I just didn't want to get into a fight and lose my
job, because I had just lost my wife and our unborn child and didn't
need to lose this job as well, because I still have our two younger sons
to provide for and I wanted them to grow up knowing their dad did
all that he could for them. Now, if it had not been for them needing
me, I would have done things just a little different."

"Just what would you have done different, sir?"

"I would have gotten fired for putting my fist against his face,
like most would have done."

"Oh, I understand now, sir. You not wanting to get fired because
of your two sons who needed you in their lives, for they had already
lost their mother. So we arrive here at your new wife's home to move
her things. You told me that she would have something for us to eat,
and I don't see any food cooking at all. I don't mean to sound rude,
but I'm hungry."

"Oh, son. You can wait until she fixes you something. You're
not going to die from starvation."

"I just might, if you keep working me like an old pack mule.
I know you are wanting to get her moved in with you today, but I
would also like something to eat today. Oh, by the way, sir. Have you
told your sons about their new stepmom?"

"No, son, I have not said anything to them about her. It was
late when I got home last night. Only you and the one you call wildflower know about us getting married yesterday. I will tell them when
they come over for dinner tonight."

"Well, what about lunch? You didn't let me have my breakfast
this morning. You were in such a hurry to get over here to your new
wife, that all I have had was a cup of coffee, and I'm doing all the
work here."

"Now, son. Don't get all upset. I will see that you get something
to eat, okay? Now, will you please get back to work?"

"No, sir, I will not. Not until I get some food in my stomach."

"Okay, son. If it will get you back to work, I will see if she will fix you a bite to eat."

"Thank you, sir, and may I also ask for a cup of water, if that's not too much to ask of you?"

"Now, son. What is with your attitude today?"

"Sir, I don't have an attitude, okay? I'm hungry and you are trying to work me like I'm your pack mule."

"Son, I have asked of her to fix you a bite to eat, and here's you a cup of water."

"Thank you very much, sir. Now I can go ahead and get this last little bit loaded on the trailer for you. Ma'am, it was very nice of you to fix such a delicious meal as this. Thank you. Sir, I have gotten all I can get onto the trailer, and it's all tied down."

"Good, son. We can now head back and get this load unloaded. You need to check on the operation that the captain has going down at the dock concerning the channel that is to be dug around the ship."

"Sir, may I ask, is she going back with us?"

"Yes, she is, son. She needs to unpack her things and get them put away. She needs these boxes to put the rest of her things in."

"Oh, okay then. Can we go now? I would like to check on the work down at the dock concerning the ship before it gets too late." We get almost halfway back to his home when the vehicle starts to cut out on us. I ask him if he had put any fuel in the tank lately.

He says, "I have not in the past week because the gauge showed full."

"Well, what is the gauge showing now, sir?"

Well! He says, "It's showing empty now and I don't understand why that is, because I have not been anywhere in it in the past two days, unless one of my sons used it and didn't tell me." I had to ask which town would be the closest, like it really mattered, because it was going to be a long walk either way. I just dropped my head in disbelief because I knew that I was going to be the one who's going to be walking back to town for fuel.

We managed to get off the highway with the trailer. I get two bottles of water and begin walking back towards the town we just came from, hoping someone would come by and give me a ride into town. Well, one came by, but he didn't stop. He just kept on going. In about ten minutes, there came someone else and he also kept going as well. I'm now thinking that I'm going to be walking all the way to town and back if someone does not stop and give me a ride. Now here comes someone else. Just maybe, he's going to stop and give me a ride into town to get the gas and bring me back to the truck. "Sir, would you be so kind as to give me a ride to town to get some gas for my friend's truck? He ran out about eight or ten miles back."

"Sure, son. Get in. I'll be more than happy to give you a ride to get fuel and bring you back to where your friends are."

"Thank you, sir. I do appreciate your help. There were two that came by earlier and didn't even stop to see if I needed help."

"Son, that's okay. I know how you feel. I myself have been where you are now and that, my friend, is the very reason I help people when I see them in need." We get the fuel and head back. He asks, "How long have you been on this journey?"

I reply with, "Sir, how do you know, I'm on a journey?"

"Oh, I talked with your friend back at the truck, and he told me about this wildflower who is with you. He said you are together on this journey in search of someone to share your lives with."

"Oh, did he now?" I asked.

"Yes, son, he did. He told me about the yellow and red rose, and even about the note you wrote explaining how you thought you felt about her."

"I asked him to keep that between me and him. Oh, just wait till we are by ourselves. I'm going to give him a piece of my mind like I never have done to anyone before."

"Wait now, son. Don't go and get all upset about him telling me this. I think it was very nice of you, trying to get her to open her heart to you, because not all men can come up with the right words to express their true feelings in the way that you did. Son, I myself think it was a very nice way for you to show her how you feel as well as having her as a friend."

"Well, thank you, sir, but that's not an excuse for him telling you about us. Did he also tell you that she is now seeing someone else?"

"No, son, he didn't. But he did say that you were going to stay and see just how things are going to work out between you two."

"Oh, I know he didn't, because I told him that just as soon as we can get the ship back out in to the ocean, I'm going to be on it." We get back to the truck with the fuel.

"Sir, once again, thank you for your help. If it had not been for you stopping and giving me a ride in to town, I don't think I would had made it."

"Son, you are welcome, and I hope that everything works out for you on your new journey in life, and may God be with you."

We get back in the truck and head toward his place, I'm sitting in the passenger seat, minding my own business. He asks, "Now, son, what is on your mind? You look upset about something."

I look over at him. "Sir, why did you tell that stranger about me?" Before he could answer me, his new wife spoke up, saying, "Son, the note was very beautiful.

He told me after the gentleman had left that you have written more like that one. I would like to read some of them, if you don't mind, son."

"No, ma'am. I don't mind you reading them. I would love to have someone like yourself read some of my writing and let me know how they sound. I have always thought about writing a book."

"Son, if it sounds anything like your note, I will most definitely let you know if it's any good or not. I love to read good books."

By this time, we are back and we get her things unloaded and put away. He asks. "Are you going to go down, and check with the captain to see how things are coming with the ship?"

"No, sir. I'm not. It has been a long day, and I'm tired. I'm going to my room and take a nap. I will go see him tomorrow."

His wife asks, "Son, are you going to let me read what you have written?"

"Yes, ma'am. I will go and get the book for you now."

"Thank you, son. I'm going to read it to John as soon as he gets done with his work in the kitchen."

"Just who is John," I ask?

"John is my husband."

"Oh," I reply. "I didn't know his name was John. I just always call him sir. May I also listen while you read it out loud just to see how it sounds when someone else is reading it?"

"Sure, son. After all, it is your writing."

She gets finished reading. She looks at me and says, "Now this is just beautiful. Are you sure you're the one who wrote this?"

"Yes, ma'am. I'm the one who wrote it."

She replies, "You are telling me that you're still single and that you can't find a nice woman to date. Don't you know women love to hear these words from you men?"

"No, ma'am, it's not that way at all. I just don't feel that they want to hear them from me."

"Well, son. If I was twenty-five years younger and single, I would be calling on you myself."

"Well, thank you again, ma'am. I do appreciate your compliment."

"Son, I see you have got a great imagination. You might want to take a course in college on journalism."

"Well, thank you, ma'am. I'm glad that you think it's that good. One day, when I find the time, I might take your advice and consider college journalism, but for now, I'm just going to keep putting my thoughts down on paper and see how they turn out."

"Son, have you thought about trying to put your writing together and have it looked at by a publishing company?"

"Well, yes, I have thought about it a time or two, but like you have said, I might need to consider taking a college course in journalism before I try getting a book published such as this one. I have no idea how a book should be laid out for a publishing company to consider publishing it for me. How would one know if he has never tried before?"

"Well now, son. That is why I said that you might want to look at taking a course in journalism. It would help you a lot in putting what you have written together. Now, as for the publishing company, I'm sure they also have people who can help put your book together for you."

"Well, ma'am, I might try doing just that once more, one of these days, when I get the money to do so."

"What did you just say, son?"

"Ma'am, I already tried getting a book published once before. I must say, it takes time, money, and a lot of hard work that goes into getting a book published, more so in the way I write, as you can see."

"Well, son. Just what is the title of you first book?"

"Ma'am, the title I originally came up with was already taken, which I didn't know, so I ended up having to name it My Life Journey as a Free, Single Man, which is okay, because I'm a free and single man, who is on a journey. "Well, ma'am and sir, I'm going to say good night once more, and I do thank you for taking time to read some of what I have written so far." I go into my room to take rest for the night, but before I do, I read the book of Luke 10. I come across these verses where Jesus was speaking to this lawyer who had asked Him what he should do to inherit eternal life.

> He said unto him, What is written in the law? how readest thou? And he answering said, Thou shalt love the Lord thy God with all thy heart, and with all thy soul, and with all thy strength, and with all thy mind, and thy neighbour as thyself. And he said unto him, Thou hast answered right: this do, and thou shalt live. But he, willing to justify himself, said unto Jesus, And who is my neighbour? And Jesus answering said, A certain man went down from Jerusalem to Jericho, and fell among thieves, which stripped him of his raiment, and wounded him, and departed, leaving him half dead. And by chance there came down a certain priest that way: and when he saw him, he passed by on the other side. And likewise a Levite, when he was at the place, came and looked on him, and passed by on the other side. But a certain Samaritan, as he journeyed, came where he was: and when he saw him, he had compassion on him, (Luke 10:26–33, KJV)

I'm going to say good night here, but before I do, I would like to ask something here. Are you doing all you can to help your neighbor by lifting them up to the Lord in your prayers, in the good times as well as the worse times in their lives?

THE WEEK OF THANKSGIVING

"**G**ood morning, Sir John, and a good morning to you also, Mrs. John. Mr. John, do you know what day of the month this is?"

"Yes, I do, son. It's the twenty-first day of November. Why do you ask?"

"Well, sir, I was thinking, if I were back home, I would be getting ready to celebrate Thanksgiving in about two days."

"What do you mean Thanksgiving, son?"

"Sir, Thanksgiving is a time we, as free people, give thanks for the freedom we have to serve our Lord Jesus Christ, who gave up his life on an ol' rugged cross, many years ago. Whoever accepted him as their personal savior would have everlasting life in His Kingdom. In about a month from Thanksgiving, we would be beginning to celebrate His birth. If it had not been for these courageous people leaving their home land in search of a new land to have the rights that we now have to worship God openly as a free country. These people were called "Pilgrims" who had a great desire to be free. So one day, this group of men decided to set sail on this ship in search of a new land to gain their freedom. I remember this one Thanksgiving, some years ago, when I, with some friends, went to the great Smoky Mountains."

"Well, did you have fun there with your friend's, son?"

"Oh, I had fun there. It's a great place to visit when you have great friends with you. If we were not out riding around and looking at all the different places that are in the beautiful Smoky Mountains, we would go to these different dinner shows that they have there, which I found to be very entertaining to watch. But this Thanksgiving year was a very cold Thanksgiving, so I went out and bought this leather jacket that I have always wanted, along with a western hat and boots that I saw which I though looked good together. So now I'm thinking that I would like to have some western shirts to go with my new hat and boots and my new leather jacket as well. So I ask the salesman if they had any western long-sleeved shirts to go with the leather jacket. The salesman replies, 'No, sir. I'm sorry. We are sold out of our western shirts, but you might find what you are looking for down at this other store that is about a mile or so down the road.' 'Oh, okay, sir,' I reply. 'Thank you for your help.'"

"Well, son, did you find what you call a western shirt?"

"Yes, sir, I did, but they were not exactly the ones I was looking for."

"Well, did you buy any?"

"Well, yes. I did find two or three that I liked."

"Well, did you find any of those lovely wildflowers anywhere in those there mountains, son??

"No, John. I didn't."

"Well, did you expect to find one in those mountains, son?"

"Well, sir. I guess not at that time, because, I simply was not looking all that hard. I had just got divorced and was not looking to fall in love all over again. I was still recovering from my first true love leaving me, if one could call it that."

"Well, son. I was under impression that you were looking to fall in love again."

"No, sir. Not anytime soon, I'm not."

"Well," John asks, "what are you going do next, son?"

"Well, John. I will tell you just what I'm going to do next, and that is I'm going to walk my happy little self down to where the ship is to see just how much longer it's going to be before we can set sail on the open sea."

John says, "Wait now. I thought you were going back to town to buy a yellow and red rose to give this wildflower who you like some much?"

"Well, no, John. It's like this, you see. I'm now seeing that she is not the one after all, so I'm not going to waste any more of my valuable time trying to convince her to go with me on this journey just to see if we have anything in common with each other outside of being all alone in this big old world."

"Well, son. Are you going to help me get my wife's things moved today?"

"Yes, sir. I'm still going to help you with that, but first, I'm going down to talk with the captain and see just how the work is coming, with them digging this great big channel around the ship."

"Oh okay. Hurry back, for we need to be going. I would love to get all her things moved in today if at all possible."

As I'm walking down to where the work is going on, I'm thinking to myself, *I'm looking forward to getting my new future started out on the open sea, but just when that is going to be?* Well, I don't know at this time in my life. Because the captain has just informed me that the work is not going exactly like he had planned.

"Well, Captain. Just what do you think we need to do to fix this problem?"

"Well," he says, "I'm not exactly sure on our part. We can call the engineers and see if they can help us out."

"Okay, sir. I will see if I can get in touch with them and ask if they can come over and assist you."

"Okay, son. That would be great."

I go back to the shop and ask Mr. John if he knows how to get in touch with the engineers.

"Why?" he asks.

"Well, the captain has just informed me that he needs their help in getting the ship back out to sea."

"Well," he replies. "Son, there has not been any engineers that I know of in this town since the shipping dock was built back in the early 1970s. Now there may be some over in the town where we are going to this morning to get her things. We can stop by and ask the owner of the track hoe if he knows of any that might be in town."

"Okay, John. We need to head that way, sir. But before we do, may I ask, have you put any fuel in the truck today?"

"Yes, I did," he replied, "but if it will put your mind at rest, son, I will stop and put more in it on the way out." We are now on the road. We are talking about the day before. He says the strange man that he had talked to about me was his younger son who he had called ten minutes after I had left walking back toward town to get fuel.

"Mr. John, may I ask? Is your name really John? I've been here now, going on six months, and I do not know your name."

"Well," he says, "no, it is not. That just the name she calls me."

"Well, Mr. John. May I ask what your real name is?

He replied, "You may also call me, Mr. John, not that I'm ashamed of my name. It's just that people find it hard to pronounce correctly, so I just tell them to call me John."

"Oh okay, Mr. John. Now I know."

"Well," he asks, "Is there anything else you might would like to know, son?"

"Well, yes. There is just one more thing. I need to ask you, John. Are you going to let me stay at your place now that you have a new wife at your shop?"

"Well, yes, son. You can stay if you need. I like having you around. Besides, we will be staying at my home as soon as I get done making the repairs."

"Thank you, John. That is very nice of you. I also like talking with you, as well." We are now at the office where we rented the track hoe. John goes in and asks the owner if he knew of any engineers still in town.

"Yes, there are, sir," the owner replied. "They are out working on the water main about two miles down the road. May I ask how is the track hoe working out for you?"

"Well, sir, it's not working out well at all. That's why we need the engineers to come and see just what needs to be done."

"Oh, okay. Good luck on getting them to go with you."

"Once again, thank you, sir. We'll stop by and ask them if they will help us." We find them and John asked the supervisor if he would mind riding out and looking at the situation that we have at the dock.

"Sure, I'll be glad to see if my men can be of help to you, but it will be after we are done here."

"Okay, sir. Thank you." We go back to her place and finish packing her things and head home for the rest of the day. "John, I'm going down to the dock to let the captain know we found the engineers and that they would be coming our way soon."

"Okay, son. Thanks."

As I'm walking down to the dock to speak with the captain regarding what the engineer's supervisor had said he would do when he gets done working on the water main, I begin to think to myself, *Am I ever going to get out of this desert anytime soon? Just how much more bad luck can come my way?* Well, as I get to where I can see the work going on, all at once, I hear this loud noise. It sounded just like two pieces of metal being struck together. I say to myself, *I sure hope that someone didn't just hit the ship with the track hoe bucket.* I see someone who I think is the captain running around to the other side of the ship. So, I also started to run to see what had just happened. As I get to the other side, I see the captain just shaking his head. "Captain, sir. Please tell me that he didn't just knock a hole in the side of the ship with the track hoe?"

He finally looks at me and says, "If it's not one thing, it's something else going on, and now this, too, has happened. I'm just one man here, and I just can't do it all by myself. Now I've got go down into the belly of the ship and see if it did puncture a hole. I'm just hoping it didn't," he says.

"Well, Captain. As I was on my way here to see you, I was thinking just how much more bad luck can come my way."

He once again looks at me and says, "Son, with this crew, you don't need to be thinking that way. If there's anything that can go wrong, it will.

Now, you came down here to tell me about what the engineer supervisor said."

"Oh, yes, sir. I almost forgot. He said that, when they are done with the repairs to the water main, he would come over and see if his men could be of help to you."

"Well, did he tell you just how long it would be before he's done with the repairs?"

"No, sir, he didn't."

"What, did you not think to ask?"

"No, I guess not, sir."

"You people," he says, "can't even think to ask questions. It would be good information to know just when someone would be coming to see if they can be of help to you or not."

"Well! Excuse me, Captain, for not being smart like you, sir! I'm going to head back to John's. I'll see you tomorrow."

He says, "Wait just a minute here, now. Just who is this John you keep speaking of?"

"Well, sir. If you must know, he's the one who owns the motor-cycle shop."

"Now, son. There's no need in getting an attitude with me."

"Well, Captain, you are the one who has the attitude here now, more so than me."

"Well, yes. I guess you are right, son. I should not have snapped at you like I did, but you've got to understand, with things having gone the way they have today, and I can't seem to fix them, well, I just take out my anger on whoever's around."

"Captain, I do understand, sir. It was just yesterday that I got upset with Mr. John. Now, Captain, what say we just take a break and head over to the coffee shop for a bite to eat and a cup of coffee?"

"Well, okay, son. That sounds like a good idea. Give me about fifteen minutes. I would first like to find out if he had knocked a hole in the side of my ship."

"Okay, Captain. I myself would like to go with you, just to see if my bad luck has gotten any worse than it has already."

"Son, you were saying that you got upset with Mr. John yesterday. May I ask what he did to get you upset with him?"

"No, sir, I don't mind you asking."

"Oh my goodness! No, no! Just what I was afraid of, son."

"What's that, Captain?"

"Son, there is water coming into the belly of the ship from somewhere. We must go farther and find the hole and see just how big and bad it really is."

"Well, Captain, if there's any water coming aboard, it's bad, is it not?"

"Not now, son. Not necessarily. We can take on water and stay afloat as long as the vacuum pumps are working properly. We have four throughout the belly of the ship for this very reason."

"Hey, Captain. Look up yonder. I see what appears to be a big dent in the side."

"Where, son?"

"Just ahead, sir. About twenty feet or so. Shine your light forward some, sir. Do you see it now?"

"Yes, son. I see it now. Let's go on up and see just how bad it is."

"Oh, Captain. It's not that big of a hole. Maybe the engineers can put a weld on it when they come to evaluate our situation."

"I hope so, son. Now let's go to the coffee shop for a bite to eat and that cup of coffee I'm in much need of, and you can tell me just what Mr. John did to you yesterday."

THE COFFEE
SHOP WAITRESS

"Good afternoon, ma'am. How are you today?"

"I'm good, thanks for asking. How are you two gentlemen?"

"Ma'am, I'm good but very hungry."

"Well, good. Now, what can I get you nice gentlemen?"

"Ma'am, I'd like to order your scrambled eggs with butter grits, a nice slice of your grilled lamb chop with a big glass of sweet tea, and a cup of coffee."

"Sir, will that be for here or to go, and do you want this to be on the same ticket order?"

"Well, ma'am, to answer the first part of your question, yes, we will be eating here. Now as for the second part of your question, that's going to depend on what the captain is going to order. He may just order your sixteen ounce ribeye steak with a lobster tail, and a loaded potato with a chef salad, and a glass of sweet tea, and a cup of coffee, but I don't know, for he didn't say. He just said he had to go to the restroom and that he'd be back in a few minutes to place his order."

"Oh okay, sir. I'll go ahead and get your order started."

"Thank you, ma'am, and can I go ahead and get my cup of coffee?"

"Sure, sir, and would you like sugar and cream to go with your coffee?"

"No, thank you, ma'am. I love my coffee just black."

"I'm sure you do, son."

"Yes, I do, when I know someone as beautiful as you are the one who prepared it."

"Oh, now, son. Are you trying to flirt with me?"

"Well now, ma'am, that all depends on how you perceive me being nice to you."

"Oh okay, sir. Then I'll go ahead and get your coffee for you. Just find yourself a table and one of the waitresses will be right out with the rest of your order."

The captain looks at me. "Now, son. What was that about?"

"Oh, Captain. It was nothing. Just nothing at all. I was just trying to be nice."

"Well, did you order for me?"

"No, sir, I didn't, because I didn't know what you wanted other than a cup of coffee. She said the other waitress should be coming with my order any time now, and you can give her your order. Oh, here she comes."

"Sir, here's your coffee."

"Thank you, ma'am. I think that the captain would like to order now. Captain? Oh, captain, the waitress is waiting for you to order. Oh my goodness. Captain, please get your eyeballs back in your head and order."

"Oh, I'm sorry, ma'am. It's just that you are so beautiful and very attractive. Are you married?"

"Well, yes, I'm married, but we are separated. I caught my husband off with another woman about three months ago, and I've been trying to get a divorce, but that takes time and money which I don't have. That is why I'm working here as a waitress, trying to make extra money to help pay for the divorce."

"Ma'am, I'm very sorry. Your husband must be one man who does not appreciate or know what he has at home."

"Well, don't be, sir. Now, may I take your order?"

"Yes, ma'am. I'll have your sixteen ounce ribeye steak and lobster-tail, with a loaded potato, a chef-salad, and to drink, a glass of sweet tea."

"How would you like your steak cooked, sir?"

"Oh, I would like it charcoal-grilled, medium well, if that's okay?"

"Will that be all, sir?"

"Yes, ma'am. For now. Thank you."

"Okay, Captain. I'll get your order request started, and son, I'll have yours out shortly."

"Thank you, ma'am."

"Now, son, you were going to tell me what Mr. John did yesterday."

"Oh, right. To make a long story short, sir"

"No, son. I would like to hear it from the beginning. Maybe it will help me get my mind off what has gone wrong today with the work down at the dock."

"Well, Captain. From the way I saw you looking at our waitress, with your eyes all popped out and your tongue hanging down to your chin, I'll say you have forgotten all about your troubles for now."

"Well, son. You've got to say, she's a very attractive and beautiful woman. Now, are you going to tell your story or not?"

"Well, let me see here. Now, I got up and walk into the kitchen yesterday morning to get something to eat and a cup of coffee before we were to go and pick up his new wife and move her things back here. So I say, 'Good morning, sir. How are you doing this morning?' and he says, 'I have already been up for some time, now. I could not sleep much at all last night for I was thinking about my new wife.'"

"Oh, hold now, son. I didn't mean you had to go that far back with your story. I'd like to know only what he did to get you upset."

"Well, Captain. You said that you wanted to hear my story as to what he did to get me upset with him, so, I'm telling it, okay? Now, first, he didn't give me time to eat. He told me that we needed to be going. She would have something at her place to eat."

"Well, son. Did she have anything fixed?"

"No, not when we got there. So I go ahead and start loading her belongings on to the trailer, and as I did so, I become hungrier than when we left that morning."

"Now, son, you got mad about that?"

"No. Now that's just the beginning of the story. He just keeps on working me like an old pack mule and didn't offer me anything to eat or drink."

"Well, son, I can see this getting you somewhat upset, working without food and all. But still, that is no reason to be mad at him."

"Sorry, sir."

"I don't mean to interrupt you two gentlemen's conversation, but here's your steak and lobster, and can I get either one of you anything else?"

"Ma'am, may I have another cup of coffee?"

"Sure, son. And what about you, Captain? Would you like anything else?"

"Oh yes, ma'am. I most definitely would, at that."

"Well, what can I get you, sir?"

"Oh, just your phone number and the time you get off work tonight."

"Sorry, sir. I'm afraid I can't give you my phone number. Now, would you be needing anything else?"

"No, ma'am. Thank you. That's all for now."

"Now, Captain. How can you be flirting with her? She's not even divorced yet and you're already hitting on her."

"Son, I'm just trying to let her know that, when she does get her divorce and she's ready to move on to the next part of her life's journey, I would be very interested in making that journey with her. Now what was the other half of the story about John telling this stranger about you?"

"Oh right. Now, let me see. Where was I? Oh yes, and he lets the truck run out of fuel and then blames it on one of his sons. Now get this part. He goes and tell's this other man about me who I have never met before. Not until yesterday, that is."

"What did he tell this strange man about you that made you so mad at him?"

"Well, Captain. I didn't find out until this morning that he was John's youngest son. Oh, I'm sorry, Captain. This is not the way I had envisioned, in the figment of my imagination, how I was going to tell you what had taken place yesterday between John and myself."

"What do you mean, son? In the figment of your imagination telling me what Mr. John did to get you upset?"

"Well, Captain. I had asked him to keep this just between me and him, but he didn't. He goes and tells his son and his new wife that I had written a very special and beautiful note to this beautiful and attractive wildflower who was, at one time, with me on this journey in search of our soulmate."

"Oh okay, son. I now understand why you got upset."

"Well, as we were headed back home, I questioned him about it. But before he could answer me, his wife spoke up, saying he had told her about more of my writing and that she would like to read them sometime to see if they came close to being as sweet and beautiful as the note."

"Well, did you let her read any of them?"

"Yes, I let her read some of them to John and myself."

"Why did she read it to you and John?"

"Well, I told her that I would like to hear how it sounded when someone else beside myself read it."

"Well, what did she say?"

"She said that it was very beautiful, and that I have a great imagination for telling a story. I also might want to consider taking a college course in journalism, which could help me in my passion for writing."

"Now, son. You have gotten my curiosity up. Would you mind if I also look at your writings as well?"

"No, I don't mind at all, Captain. I would like to know what people think about my writing. I will meet you here tomorrow for lunch and you can read over them then. Now, Captain, you must promise me one thing. You will be completely honest with me and let me know what you think. Do you promise, Captain? Yes or no?"

"Yes, son. I promise to be completely honest with you on how they sound."

"Okay then, sir. Thank you for your promise. I'm going to head on back and see what Mr. John has got going on."

"Oh, son. There's no telling with him and his new wife. It may be something you might not want to know about, if you know what I mean."

"Oh! Captain, you didn't need to go there. Are you ready to go?"

"No, son. I think I'm going to just hang out here a little while longer and talk with this very beautiful waitress and see if I can talk her into giving me her phone number and home address before I leave. She has got my blood boiling tonight. Man, she knows she hot."

"Okay, Captain. Suit yourself, or she might just actually shoot you herself. I'll see you tomorrow."

"What do you mean, son? She might shoot me?"

"Well, Captain. If you slap her backside once more, she just might do that."

"Oh no. Son, women love for men to slap their backside. It lets them know you find them attractive."

"Well, if you say so, Captain."

"Oh, I will say so, son. I know firsthand they love this kind of attention. You just need to stick with me for a week. I'll show you things you've never see in your life. I'll have all kinds of women falling all over you about an hour after meeting them."

"Well, okay, Captain. Like I said, I'll see you tomorrow."

"Good evening, Mr. and Mrs. John. How are you two doing this afternoon?"

"Oh, son. We are good as far as everything goes. How about yourself?"

"Well, ma'am. To be honest with you, I'm not all that happy right now."

"What are you unhappy about, son? And may I also ask, just where have you been all day?"

John speaks up. "Have you forgotten, son? We were to go get the rest of her things moved today."

"No, sir, I did not forget that. With all due respect, sir, you are the one who must have forgotten where I told you I was going this morning. I know you are seventy-eight years old, and that you have just remarried, and that you are still on your honeymoon, but do you not recall me telling you I was going down to the dock to see the captain to let him know we had found the engineers and that the supervisor said he would come over as soon as he gets done with the water main?"

"Oh yes, you are right. I'm sorry, son. I guess I did forget you telling me that you were going to see the captain. Now, what are you unhappy about?"

"Well, John, as I almost get there, I hear this loud noise. It sounded just like two pieces of metal being slapped together. Then I see the captain take off running to the other side of the ship, so I also ran to see what happened."

"Well, son. What happened?"

"To be truthfully honest with you, because I didn't see it happen, the captain said that the track hoe operator hit the ship with the bucket, knocking a hole in its side."

"Just how big of a hole did it make?"

"Oh, it's a nice size one. We believe the engineers will be able to weld it when they get here."

"Well, son, I understand why you would be unhappy about this, because I know you were looking forward of getting out of this desert and it being your only way, but son, you must understand that this, too, will pass."

"Yes, ma'am. You are so right. Thank you for reminding me that this, too, will surely pass. I'm going to say goodnight now."

"Son, before you go. May we speak with you for a few minutes about something?"

THE UNEXPECTED MOMENT

"Sure, I don't mind. I really don't have anything else to do, that's if you don't mind me having a cup of coffee while we talk."

"Oh no, son. We don't mind at all, do we, John?"

"Aye, sounds like a great idea to me, but I am thinking something stronger than coffee."

"Oh now, John, you don't need anything stronger than coffee tonight.

"Well, Mom, you know it's helps me to sleep better."

"Well now, John, who says that we will be doing any sleeping tonight?"

"Oh, Mom. Are you feeling frisky again?"

"Oh, hold on now, you two. Why don't we all just go into the kitchen and I'll fix us a cup, okay?"

"Now, son. We have been talking about your writing and we have come up with some ideas on how you might be able to pay for these college courses in journalism, that's if you even decide to pursue a career in journalism."

"Well, Ma'am. Like I had already mentioned to you before, I had already written one book and I don't really have that much confidence in it. As for as anyone liking it or even if it will sell that well, I'm just not that sure of myself right now, with the way my life has been going."

"Now, son, we know that you are heartbroken and all, but just listen to our ideas, okay?"

"Yes, Ma'am. I will listen to your ideas, but at the same time, I'm starting to think just like Mr. John. I may be the one who will be needing something stronger to drink than coffee before this conversation is over with you acting the way you are. Okay. Now, just what are your ideas?"

"Well, here's one way we came up with. You can join the military. We heard they give their service members this thing called student grants or something. Iit's to help them in paying for college tuition."

"Wait just a minute now. Did you just say military?"

"Yes, I did, son. Why? Is there something wrong with being in the military, son? Well, no. Not that I can think of, outside of spending most of your time away from the ones you love the most."

"Well, son, that's just one way. Here's one you might like to consider."

"Okay, and just what would that be, Mrs. John?"

"Now, son. There is no need for you getting an attitude. We're just trying to come up with ways to help you because we like what you have written from your first manuscript. If your book is going to be anything like this, you may just have something going for you."

"Well, I'm sorry, Mrs. John. I didn't mean for it to sound as if I was not interested in hearing your ideas." At the same time, I'm thinking to myself, *Yeah right. You say you like my writing. Nobody even likes to hear what I have to say because of the way I pronounce my words in a sentence.* "Now, you were saying, Mrs. John?"

"Son, you might be able to get with another well-known author who has more experience in writing. No matter whoever he or she may be, they could teach you more about how to structure your thoughts on paper and make them more presentable and interesting to read. Now, we both decided to save what we think is the best one for last."

I'm thinking, *Good. We have now reached what you two think is the best one. I'm just dying from all the excitement and expectation of knowing what it's going to be.*

"Now, son. Listen to me very carefully here. Mr. John and I are up in age and may not have much longer to live here on Mother Earth, so with this in mind, we would like to help you out by offering you our assistance in any way we can in getting you a college degree in journalism, because we believe if you push yourself hard enough with the imagination that you have, you will have a great chance at exceeding with your writing. Now what do you say to that, son?"

"I would say a double wow— no wait— that would be a quadruple wow! Thank you both for your vote of confidence in me."

"Well, son. No matter how much confidence anybody else may or may not have in your ability to write or do anything else, if you set your mind to achieve in life, you can. You've just got to believe in yourself and push a little bit harder."

"Once again, thank you both, and I must excuse myself. I've got to go to the restroom. Oh, and goodnight."

"Well, John. Do you think he will buy off on what I just told him?"

"I don't know now, Mama. That boy sure appears to be set in his ways, and it's going to be hard to convince him. I think he has a mighty hard head like an old billy goat. You know just how hard-headed they are."

"Yes, John, I do. You don't have to remind me. I just married one. Here, John look at this one. I found it in his room today when I was cleaning. He must have written it this morning."

"Now, Mama. You know it's not right to be reading someone else's writing without their permission."

"Oh, just go ahead and read it, John. If he had not wanted it read, he would not have left it on the bed for me to see. He knows that I clean his room every day."

"Well, okay then, Mama. Since you put it that way. I guess it's okay just this once. Maybe, if you think."

"John, who's being hardheaded like an old billy goat now? Now, just give it here. I'll read it to you."

"No, Mama. I'm going to read it. Just let me get my glasses. Do you think he may have taken this part out of his first book also?"

"No, John. I don't think so, because look at the date he has written on it."

"Oh right, Mama."

THE EIGHTH OF DECEMBER: FIRST SNOW OF THE YEAR

As I stand here, looking out across the wide-open plain as it becomes covered with snow, I'm reminded of my life as a singer without salvation until the day Jesus came and gave his blood to wash my sins away. As for the sprigs that I see which have not become covered, oh Lord, my God, they remind me that I am a sinner who needs Jesus's blood applied to my life as I travel down this long rugged road on this journey in life which I have found myself on in search of my one true love. Thank You, my God the Father, who has given

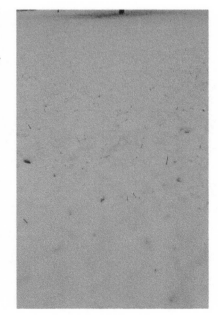

unto me the wisdom and knowledge to recognize that, as a sinner, I needed Thy Son, Jesus, in my life.

"Now, John, how does that sound to you?"

"Son, it's okay. Just a little off the wall, you might say, but I'm thinking it could sound better. What do you think, Mama? After all, you're more of an expert on writing letters than I am. Mama, do you rememberthe first love letter you wrote me back in school?"

"Oh now, John, that was so many years ago, and I have forgotten all about those days. Well, maybe it could use just a little correction here and there. It wouldn't change the meaning all that much."

"Goodnight Mr. and Mrs. John."

"Goodnight to you also, son. See you in the morning."

"Oh, Mrs. John. Have you seen one of my papers that I had left here on the bed this morning?"

"Which one would that be, son?"

"The one that says the eighth of December, the first snow of the year."

"Oh that one."

"Yes, ma'am, that one. Do you recall just where you put it when you made the bed this morning?"

"Yes, son, we have it in here. We just finished reading it."

"Oh, okay. Thanks."

"Good morning, everyone. Hope you've all gotten yourselves a good night's rest, because today is going to be a very busy one."

"Yes, son. You are right about that. We got to get over to her old place and get the rest of her things moved over here, because she has someone who is wanting to buy that house as soon as she gets all of her things out: and then, when we get that done for the day, I got to go check on my place to see how much longer it's going to be before we can move back in there. So with that, we need to be on our way right now."

"You need to hold on here now, Mr. John. We are not going anywhere until I have had my coffee and something to eat, because last time, I didn't get anything to eat until well after midday.

Okay, I'm ready now, Mr. John, if you are.

"Son, I have been ready to get this day started way before you ever decided that you were going to get your lazy self up this morning."

"Oh, you have, have you? Then why didn't you already have breakfast prepared for me if you were in that much of a hurry to get this day started now, old goat?"

"Now, son. There is no need in you calling me an old goat."

"Oh, there's not, is there? Then why did you just call me lazy?"

"What are you two arguing about? I hear you always down the hall."

"Oh, Mama, it's nothing. I'm just being truthful with him, that I didn't know just what he may have wanted for breakfast, and he called me an old goat."

"Well, don't you two think you need to be going? You are burning valuable time. Now go."

"Yes, ma'am."

Now I'm thinking that I can really see just how this day is going to go from here.

AIRBORNE TRUCK

"Son, do you have any more stories you can tell me about yourself as we head to pick up her things?"

"Why do you ask John?"

"Well, son. I like the way you tell things that have taken place in your life, and I would like to hear more of them, and it helps pass time."

"Well, okay. Here's one for you. I was on my way home from work, one morning. Me and one of my brothers— "

"Oh now, wait. You are telling me that you and your brother rode back and forth to work together? What, did you and your brother work at the same place?"

"Yes, sir. We both worked the night shift at a sawmill for about ten years. That is, until I switched to the day shift."

"What kind of work did you do at this sawmill, son?"

"Well, I started out doing whatever my supervisor needed done. From pulling lumber off the pull chain, stacking them in the buggies for the forklift, to picking them up and taking them to the stripper. From there, I work my way up the ladder to later become a lumber grader. As I made my way up that ladder from off the pull chain, I ran the package maker. From there, I ran the trim saws. Now, part of the duties of the operator was to perform maintenance on the saws at the end of the shift, which made a long night."

"How long did you work at this sawmill?"

"I worked there fifteen and a half years. Now, can I finish telling the story please?"

"Oh yes, please do."

"Thank you. Now, the old road that we had to travel was in the process of being rebuilt. Well, this one afternoon, when we wen t to work, the road was okay to travel."

"Wait just a minute, son. You were saying that this story took place in the morning time. Now you're saying this afternoon. Now, which is it going to be: morning or afternoon?"

"Yes, I did say morning first and then the afternoon, simply because I'm trying to set the stage for how the road condition had changed from the time we went to work that afternoon to the next morning, when we got off from work, so you would know why I said 'airborne truck.'"

"What? Did you own a truck, son? Well, just what kind was it? Was it a big truck or a little one? What color was the truck? Was it an old truck?"

"Man, you know what? I'm not going to tell you this story."

"Why, son, why?"

"You've got to ask why? Because I just won't, that's why. You just keep driving. I'm going to write about something else that just came across my mind."

"And what would that be, son?"

"I'm not going to say. You just got to wait until I get it written."

"Well, okay, son. Work your brain and see just what you can come up with that would be interesting for someone like myself to read, while I'm doing all the driving there and back."

"Well, sir, I'm guessing I'll be the only one doing all the loading and unloading of your wife's things."

"Now, son. Are you forgetting that I'm seventy-eight years old and I can't lift all that much weight?"

"John, just drive and stop interrupting my train of thought. I'm trying to get this written down before I forget it."

I find myself standing here, looking out across the snow-covered ground. It sparkles like silver glitter. I'm reminded of a time, not long ago, when I first considered your beautiful eyes as they sparkled like the stars of heaven's midnight skies. Oh, only if you knew just how your sparkling eyes concern my soul when I look softly into them. Oh, for now, I can only dream, in the figments of my imagination, of the day when I'm able to find my way back to you, my long awaiting love. Oh, only if you knew how my soul yearns to hold you once again, close in my arms, as I gaze softly into your eyes as they change into different shades of colors like a snowflake as it floats though the cold winter breeze. Heaven, which it came, reflects its beautiful rays of light upon it. As I slowly stroke your long autumn hair, my fingers find themselves working towards the back of your neck. My love causes friction, which makes the sparkle in your eyes shine brighter that the sun shines upon a falling snowflake. It starts a fire within my soul, which only an amount of snow can cover. As I gently pull you closer, our lips begin to touch, making the flames within my soul burn that much hotter, melting me to my knees for your love alone.

"Mrs. John, would you mind reading over this and then telling me how it sounds to you?

Okay, Mrs. John. Now that we have all your things put away, will there be anything else you would like for me to do before I head down to meet the captain for lunch?"

"No, son. I don't know of anything else right off the top of my head. Oh, by the way, your note sounds very lovely, son. I will say you do have a way with words. I don't know how you come up with the sayings that you do. They are very beautiful. You can go ahead on down and meet the captain for lunch."

"Thank you, Mrs. John. It's very nice of you to think so. I will see you at supper tonight."

MEETING WITH
THE CAPTAIN

"Good afternoon, Captain. How has your day gone so far?"

"Well now, son. Almost as bad as the way it ended yesterday, but I was able to put a stop to the horse playing that the guys were doing."

"Oh? May I ask how you did that, Captain?"

"I just threatened to let each one of them go if I caught them horse playing around my ship again."

"Oh okay. Did that work?"

"Yes, they didn't tear anything else up today."

"Oh good, then. Shall we go on in and find a table? I brought some of my writing with me for you to look at."

"Oh right. Your paper. I was going to tell you that I had stopped by last night and spoke with Mr. and Mrs. John about your writing."

"Oh. You stopped by and asked someone else about my writing, did you? I'm guessing you didn't believe me? Hmm? And why is that, Captain."

"Oh no, son. It's not like that at all. Now, just hear me out. I don't know anything about you yet. It's been only a week or so that we met, and I wanted to know what they had to say about your writing before I also gave you my opinion on them."

"Well then, in that case, Captain. Just what did they have to say about what they read?"

"Well now, you must first promise me you will not go back and tell them everything that I have told you, they said."

"Oh, now I got to know what they said now that you have asked me to promise."

"Well, do you promise?"

"Well now, Captain, I'm going think about this while you read, and like I told them, this is just some parts I tied together from my first manuscript."

"Good afternoon, gentlemen. Are you ready to order?"

"Yes, ma'am. I'll have just a small chef salad with ranch dressing."

"What would you have to drink, sir? A glass of sweet tea with a lemon, please."

"Will there be anything else?"

"No, ma'am."

"What can I get you, Captain?"

"I'll just have a cheeseburger with fries, and to drink, I'll also have sweet tea."

"What kind of cheese would you like on your burger?"

"Do you have goat cheese?"

"I think we just might, at that. Captain, may I ask? Just what you are reading there?"

"Ma'am, it's just something he has written from his first book. He said he took parts from different chapters and put them together, so, I asked if he minded if I could look at it, and so far, son, I must say it's very impressive the way you used your imagination in writing this."

"Thank you, Captain, for saying that. There are some who think I'm not capable of writing a book, just because of my inability to pronounce certain words and getting them spelled correctly. That is why I don't have much confidence in my only ability, but to just prove a point, I left some mistakes in the first book."

"Well, son," she asked, "do you mind if I also look at it as well?"

"Sure, ma'am. I don't mind at all, that is, if you've got the time to do so after the captain is done."

"Okay, thanks. I'll go ahead and get your order started and bring your tea over to you. Here's you order, sir. Now, Captain, are you finished reading his papers?"

"Oh yes, ma'am. I'm done."

"Okay. May I take it back with me? I'm going on break in about five minutes."

"Sure, just bring it back when you are done."

"Now, Captain. May I share my thoughts with you on something that might sound just a little off the wall to you?"

"Yeah, sure. What's on your mind, son."

"Well, it's like this. When I start to feel that people are making fun of my inability in doing things, like they think that they are so much better, I remind myself of reading this in Isaiah 64:6–12.

> But we are all as an unclean thing, and all our righteousnesses are as filthy rags, and we all do fade as a leaf, and our iniquities, like the wind, have taken us away. And there is none that calleth upon thy name, that stirreth up himself to take hold of thee: for thou hast hid thy face from us, and hast consumed us, because of our iniquities. But now, O Lord thou art our father, we are the clay, and thou our potter, and we all are the work of thy hand. Be not wroth very sore, O Lord, neither remember iniquity forever: behold, see, we beseech thee, we are all thy people. Thy holy citirs are a wilderness, Zion is a wilderness, Jerusalem a desolation. Our holy and our beautiful house, where our fathers praised thee, is burned up with fire: and our pleasant things are laid waste. Wilt thou refrain thyself for these things, O Lord? Wilt thou hold thy peace, and afflict us very sore? (Isaiah 64:6–12, KJV)

"Now, son, you did write this from within your heart?"

"Yes, ma'am. I did."

"May I ask? Are you married?"

"No, ma'am. I'm not."

"Are you dating anyone right now?"

"Once again, no, ma'am. I've not seen anyone at this time. Now, may I ask why you ask these questions?"

"Well, son. A man who thinks and talks like this should know that we women love for our man to say these kinds of things to us."

"Yes, ma'am. I know, but like I said in the beginning of my journey, I have not yet met that one woman who holds the other half of my soul, who would like to hear them from me."

"Son, you do know that there lots of single women out there in this old world who are waiting to meet someone like yourself. And I'm hoping, in a few more months, I'm going to be one of them, and if you are still around, I would like for you to take me out one night for dinner, and maybe a movie, to see if there is any chemistry between us."

Wow! Now I sure didn't see that coming. "Thank you, ma'am. I will keep that in mind, but like you said, that's if I'm still around when you do become available again. Now, ma'am and Captain, I appreciate your honesty as to what you think about my writing, for there is much more I would love to talk with you about, but I'm must say goodnight for now, and until we meet again my friends, may God keep his loving arms around you forevermore.

"Good evening, Mr. and Mrs. John. How are you doing?"

"Oh hi, son. I'm guessing one could say we are doing good. How about you?"

"You could say that I am doing good as well."

"Well, son, may I ask if you are going to tell us what the captain had to say about your writing?"

"Ma'am, he said that he also agreed with you and Mr. John. I do have a way of using my imagination in telling a story, and he feels that I need to consider taking classes in creative writing."

"See, son. You may think that we're just pulling your leg on how good your writing is, but now that you have let the captain read it and he agreed with us, what are you going to do?"

"Well, ma'am, I'm just going to wait until my knowledge."

"You could go ahead and get a skill that could help you out in any kind of career: for you will never know if you don't try."

"Yes, ma'am, you are right I never, in my wildest dreams, thought that I could write something that someone thought was good enough to be published. But I must say, I do have my own doubts from what others have said to me about it."

"Now, son. You do know, from within your own heart, that there or people in this world who will look down on you, no matter what you do."

"Yes, ma'am. I know that we are to keep our adversaries close and be a light unto them, letting them see our own faith in Christ, and not become a stumbling block unto them. They themselves are out to set snares before us and try to get us to fall into their trap, becoming like them. It appears as if they themselves have become lovers of their own flesh, being backbiters and haters of others by spreading vicious rumors of one's misfortunes or anything that they can think of to take themselves out from under the spot light of their own incompetent, unrighteous acts. Now, may I ask? Is this the right way in which someone who considers themselves to be a Christian should conduct themselves? With this question in mind, I'm going to ask of you to consider the book of Romans 2 and read it for yourself.

Here, once again, Clay finds himself to be in deep thought, using a figment of his imagination on where he might go next in this journey of life to look for the one true love who, he feels, holds the other half of his soul. Will he be able to find the wildflower in the next leg of his journey? Only time will tell when the ship, itself, will be able to, once again, set sail back out upon the open sea. It may take him on a journey unlike any he has ever found himself on. When will this new journey of his begin? No one knows for certain.

ABOUT THE AUTHOR

Clay Mills is a returning author who has found himself inspired to write these short stories about this journey. that he calls "searching for true love." He grew up in a small town in the south part of the United States and is a high school graduate from Clara High School. Clay has two grown children and is blessed with one grandchild. He is surrounded by very supportive friends who encourage him to continue pursuing his passion of writing. With this, Clay thanks each and every one who reads his work from the bottom of his heart. May the Lord our God bless you as he has the one who has written this book.